Engaging Exceptional Students

A PRIMER FOR COLLABORATION AND POSITIVE CLASSROOM MANAGEMENT

THERESA A. OCHOA, PH.D. and
AERIN M. WELCH, PH.D.

Indiana University Bloomington

 cognella®

SAN DIEGO

Bassim Hamadeh, CEO and Publisher
Angela Schultz, Senior Field Acquisitions Editor
Gem Rabanera, Senior Project Editor
Abbey Hastings, Production Editor
Jess Estrella, Senior Graphic Designer
Kylie Bartolome, Licensing Coordinator
Natalie Piccotti, Director of Marketing
Kassie Graves, Senior Vice President, Editorial
Jamie Giganti, Director of Academic Publishing

Cover image: Copyright © 2011 iStockphoto LP/TerryJ.
    Copyright © 2014 iStockphoto LP/kali9.
    Copyright © 2016 iStockphoto LP/FatCamera.
    Copyright © 2019 iStockphoto LP/skynesher.
    Copyright © 2019 iStockphoto LP/enjoynz.
    Copyright © 2022 iStockphoto LP/RichLegg.

Printed in the United States of America.

3970 Sorrento Valley Blvd., Ste. 500, San Diego, CA 92121

This book is dedicated to Larry Levy, my husband, for his unconditional support, bountiful edits, and delicious salads at noon.

—Theresa A. Ochoa

We thank our past and future students for allowing us to learn about ways to make classrooms radiate love and acceptance for all students.

—Aerin M. Welch

CONTENTS

ACTIVE LEARNING

This book has interactive activities available to complement your reading.

Your instructor may have customized the selection of activities available for your unique course. Please check with your professor to verify whether your class will access this content through the Cognella Active Learning portal (http://active.cognella.com) or through your home learning management system.

Introduction to Students with Disabilities and the School-to-Prison Pipeline

By Theresa A. Ochoa, PhD; Aerin M. Welch, PhD; Susan L. Roberts, EdD; and Shelly S. Mclean Bent, MA

This chapter begins with an introduction that focuses on the risk of incarceration faced by students with disabilities and the important role teachers play in their academic success or failure. Academic failure will in turn heighten the risk that students with disabilities will drop out of school and get involved in conflict with law enforcement. Students with disabilities are especially vulnerable to incarceration when they are not attending school. Therefore, it is crucial for future educators to understand how their response to student behavior in the classroom impacts the educational and emotional well-being of students with disabilities. Classroom teachers who create safe and effective learning environments for students, even when they misbehave, are protecting all students from school failure and incarceration.

In the introduction chapter, readers will:

- Gain awareness of the *School-to-Prison-Pipeline* (STPP) and the circumstances that lead students to incarceration;
- Understand the unintentional negative role the general educator might play in the STPP when students are removed from the classroom because of disruptive behavior;
- Identify which students with disabilities are at risk for the STPP;
- Identify factors that increase risk of being removed from the general education classroom.

All Future Educators
Student behavior is more than a reaction to a directive or situation. Consider the underlying psychological and even medical factors that may influence behavior.

Elementary General Education
Removal from the classroom results in missed instruction and can impair the learning of foundational skills, which are the building blocks for all future learning.

Secondary General Education
Students with disabilities with a history of removal from class may be significantly behind their same-grade peers academically and may have little motivation to engage in instruction.

Special Education
Student behavior that results in classroom removal may require more than just behavior intervention. Lost time in instruction and loss of learning in the need for skill remediation.

Undergraduates Interested In Disability Laws
Civil rights are legal rights or privileges awarded by the federal government. When individuals are discriminated against based on their membership to a particular group of people, these individuals are denied their civil rights.

After reading the introduction, readers will be able to:

- Identify and discuss the various factors involved in the STPP;
- Identify the terms for STPP, ODR, SLD, and EBD;
- Discuss the relationship between student misbehavior in the classroom and the role general education teachers play in the STPP.

The School-to-Prison Pipeline

The term ***School-to-Prison Pipeline*** (STPP) describes a process by which some students go from school to a juvenile correctional facility (American Civil Liberties Union [ACLU], 2019). Attention among educators and policy makers to juvenile incarceration has grown because of concerns over mass incarceration practices in the United States of America (US). At the juvenile correctional confinement level, it is estimated that about 50,000 minors between the ages of 12 to 18 are in correctional confinement on any given day (Slaughter, 2018). The strongest predictor of incarceration as an adult is incarceration as an adolescent (Oshima et al., 2010). Therefore, it is critical to examine the student factors, family factors, school factors, and the community and law enforcement factors associated with juvenile incarceration.

In cases where students engage in extreme violence, they can be removed immediately from school and placed directly in custody. However, these cases are the exception rather than the rule. The path to incarceration is typically a multistage process. Figure 1.1 show the steps in the process from school to incarceration, or the STPP. The first two steps in the "pipeline" begins when a student engages in overt disruptive classroom behavior and is removed from the classroom (as depicted in

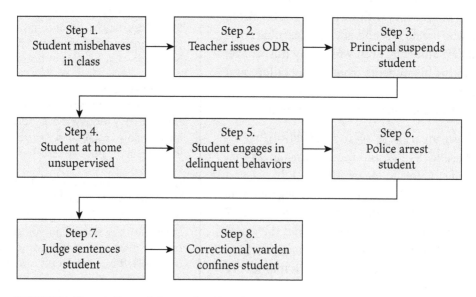

FIGURE 1.1 Steps in the path from school to prison

Steps 1 and 2 in Figure 1.1). Frequent removal from the classroom impacts academic performance and, in most cases, does not resolve the misbehavior. There is no evidence confirming that teachers maliciously exclude students with disabilities from instruction in the general education classroom. Nonetheless, the fact remains that students with disabilities were more likely to receive **office discipline referrals** (ODRs) compared to their non-disabled peers (Skiba et al., 1997). Regardless of intent, it is harmful to remove students with disabilities from instruction through ODRs. Students do not learn appropriate classroom behavior in the school principal's office. All that is gained by removing the student who misbehaves is temporary relief from interruptions by the student.

> *Students do not learn appropriate classroom behavior in the school principal's office. All that is gained by removing the student who misbehaves is temporary relief from interruptions by the student.*

Increases in disruptive classroom behavior can lead to further disciplinary problems. Repetitive removal from the classroom diminishes not only instructional time, but also increases the likelihood that the student will be suspended from school (as indicated in Step 3 in Figure 1.1). Many schools use suspension and expulsion as part of their schoolwide discipline practices (Fenning & Rose, 2007). Harsh disciplinary practices used in schools, such as zero tolerance policies, that remove students from instruction for misbehavior have been correctly argued to resemble disciplinary models used in law enforcement (Skiba et al., 1997). Under zero tolerance policies, schools treat minor and severe behavior similarly, resulting not only in suspension from school but also in the increased involvement of law enforcement in managing student disruptive behavior in schools.

Once students are suspended, they typically stay at home during the school day (Step 4 in Figure 1.1). In many cases of out-of-school suspension, students are unsupervised at home. Students who are unsupervised at home have a higher risk of engaging in delinquent behavior by themselves or with peers (Step 5 in Figure 1.1). Understandably, many parents cannot remain at home when their child is suspended or expelled from school because they must attend to their employment responsibilities. Delinquent behavior, in turn, heightens the risk of being arrested (Step 6 in Figure 1.1) and can eventually lead to a judge making the decision to remand the student to a juvenile correctional facility (Steps 7 and 8 in Figure 1.1).

Students with Disabilities Who Are at Risk for Incarceration

Students with disabilities are overrepresented in juvenile correctional facilities (Bergh & Cowell, 2013). In fact, students with disabilities make up only about 14% of the general school population (National Center for Educational Statistics [NCES], 2021), yet about 33.4% of youth in confinement had a disability (Quinn et al., 2005). However, not all students with disabilities share equal risk of incarceration. Quinn et al. (2005) reported that the most common disabilities represented in the juvenile corrections system were students with **emotional and behavioral disabilities** (EBD; 47.7%)

and **specific learning disabilities** (38.6%). Only 5% of students with disabilities in public school settings were students with emotional and behavioral disabilities (NCES, 2021), compared to the 47.7% in juvenile correctional facilities. Similarly, albeit to a lesser degree, only 34% of students with a disability in public school settings were students with specific learning disabilities, while 38.6% of incarcerated youth had a specific learning disability. Although students with disabilities were at an increased risk of receiving an ODR, students with EBDs were two to three times more likely to receive ODRs than any other student, with or without disabilities (Skiba et al., 1997; Whitford, 2017). Students with specific learning disabilities also received ODRs at higher rates than their non-disabled peers (Krezmien et al., 2006). What characteristic in students with EBD and SLD increases their risk of ODRs?

Characteristics of Students with Disabilities and Challenging Behavior

Students with disabilities, especially students with emotional and behavioral disabilities, are more likely to engage in behaviors that are perceived as deserving removal from the classroom. As will be clear in subsequent chapters, behavior dysregulation is a common challenge among students with disabilities. Each category of disability included in the Individuals with Disabilities Education Improvement Act (IDEA, 2004) is recognized by a unique set of criteria. However, there are some overlapping characteristics (see Chapter 6), including deficits in executive functioning and interpersonal communication skills. Deficits in interpersonal communication skills for students with disabilities may have been a potential source of frustration for teachers and other children, which could have inhibited the development of meaningful relationships and sense of belonging (Packman & Bratton, 2003). Persistent trouble relating to others or not being able to interpret nonverbal cues from others can lead students to develop internalizing problems, such as low self-esteem, anxiety, depression, and withdrawal, as well as externalizing behaviors such as social awkwardness, impulsivity, and aggression (Packman & Bratton, 2003). Deficits in communication skills among students with disabilities can result in continued teacher and peer rejection. Externalizing behaviors can be considered defiant or disrespectful when viewed by the teacher as behavior choice rather than a manifestation of disability. In sum, friction between teachers and students due to disruptive classroom behavior can heighten risk of removal from the general education classroom.

> *When students receive an ODR, it is based in part on student behavior, and in part on how teachers interpret said behavior.*

General Education Teachers and School Discipline

As noted previously, intentional malevolent discrimination is unlikely to be the reason students with disabilities may end up in correctional confinement instead of being in school. Teachers may remove students from the classroom in response to student misbehavior as a means of gaining or maintaining control of the classroom. Lack of awareness by teachers of how disabilities might affect classroom behavior also likely affects the decision to remove a student from the classroom through an ODR when a student misbehaves. It is important for educators to understand what precipitates student behavior in the classroom, such as home life, previous school experiences, and relationships with adults and peers.

To appropriately respond to the classroom behaviors of students, it is important to understand what is driving student misbehavior or what is happening to students that is causing them to behave in inappropriate manners. Is someone talking in a tone that could be perceived as threatening? Is something happening in the classroom that is triggering a behavior? Is the child feeling afraid or defeated? All these factors can interfere with learning and be correlated to student disruptive classroom behavior. Research indicates that many general education teachers lack effective classroom management skills (Fenning & Rose, 2007). However, these teachers are responsible for classroom management and responding to student misbehavior.

Fenning and Rose (2007) found that many teachers are limited in behavior management skills. Most often, students receive ODRs for behaviors that are subjective in nature, such as defiance and disrespecting teachers (Gregory et al., 2010; Skiba et al., 1997; Vincent et al., 2012). These behaviors are all filtered through teachers' attitudes and beliefs about what is and is not acceptable behavior. This could indicate that when students receive an ODR, it is based in part on student behavior and in part on how teachers interpret said behavior. Oliver and Reschly (2010) found that comprehensive classroom management procedures, including those that focused on prevention (structured strategies, rules, classroom expectations, and routines) were missing from teacher preparation courses. Without the skills necessary to create a learning environment that is structured and proactive, rather than reactive and punitive, challenging behavior from students who cannot control their behavior may continue to intensify. In response to disruptive classroom behavior, if the teacher is ill equipped to handle disruptive classroom behavior from a student, a teacher's response, understandably, is to eliminate the problem by removing the student from the classroom.

Responding to Disruptive Classroom Behavior

Teachers need to develop skills to create a hospitable and safe learning environment where students—all students—can learn ways to attend to instruction as well as beginning and finishing tasks (Simonsen et al., 2008). In elementary school and secondary school, students need interaction with caring teachers who support the development of their pro-social and adaptive skills. Other students who misbehave need the support of their teachers to learn to behave in an appropriate manner, since it is unlikely that they will develop skills in the school principal's office. It is important that teachers demonstrate belief in positive outcomes for the student. For this reason, it is essential for teachers to learn about how disabilities impact students' classroom behavior. Without this understanding and instructional bandwidth, or what Gerber (2005) refers to as instructional tolerance, teachers may be unable to reach students with learning and behavioral disabilities. Instructional tolerance is influenced by teachers' knowledge, understanding, and skills of what influences student behavior and of appropriate in-classroom behavioral management strategies and techniques.

> *It is essential for teachers to learn about how disabilities impact students' classroom behavior.*

Additionally, it is important to help teachers develop strong classroom management skills. Without effective classroom management skills, teacher focus and attention may primarily be on student misbehavior rather than on academic learning (Cook et al., 2007). This could result in poorer student learning outcomes and an increase in the negative perceptions and lower expectations teachers have of students who exhibit learning and behavioral problems. That in turn can increase student disruptive behaviors and reduce teacher effectiveness in the classroom (Brophy & Good, 1984). Providing teachers with the knowledge of factors that may influence student behavior could facilitate an increase in teacher tolerance, and influence, in positive ways, how teachers respond to student misbehavior. Preparing teachers in effective classroom management strategies could also help reduce student disruptive behavior.

Summary

In Chapter 1, the school factors that increase the risk of incarceration, such as ODRs and out-of-school suspension, were discussed. In most cases the removal of students from the classroom was most likely not due to intentional malice, but rather reflects the need for effective behavioral classroom management strategies and better understanding of the driving forces behind student behavior.

Test Your Knowledge

1. In your own words, define **STPP**.
2. What do **ODR**, **SLD**, and **EBD** stand for?
3. Which group of students with disabilities is more likely to be incarcerated?
4. Discuss why educators might remove students exhibiting problematic behavior from the classroom.
5. Identify the steps in the **school-to-prison process**.

Apply Your Knowledge

In chapters 1 through 7, you will be asked to use the ASK-READ-TELL (ART) method to answer critical thinking questions. ART is a form of reading intervention that guides students to focus on relevant information to answer unique questions.

Ask

Ask yourself the following question to help guide your reading.

- What is the relationship between student misbehavior in the classroom and general education teachers' responses in the STPP (removal from the classroom)?

Read

Read the following sections.

- General Education Teachers and School Discipline & Responding to Disruptive Classroom Behavior (p. 4)

Tell

Tell your response.

- Given what you now know about the link between school discipline and the risk of incarceration, what are some steps educators can take to address student misbehavior without sending the students out of their classroom to be disciplined?

References

American Civil Liberties Union (ACLU). (2019). School-to-prison pipeline. Retrieved from American Civil Liberties Union website: https://www.aclu.org/issues/racial-justice/race-and-inequality-education/school-prison-pipeline

Bergh, B., & Cowell, J. (2013). Discipline referral outcomes: Meeting the needs of students. *Education Leadership Review, 14*(3), 12–21.

Brophy, J., & Good, T. L. (1984). Teacher behavior and student achievement. Occasional Paper No. 73. *Institute for Research on Teaching, College of Education, Michigan State University,* 1–174.

Cook, B. G., Cameron, D. L., & Tankersley, M. (2007). Inclusive teachers' attitudinal ratings of their students with disabilities. *Journal of Special Education, 40*(4), 230–238. Retrieved from http://www.proedinc.com

Fenning, P., & Rose, J. (2007). Overrepresentation of African American students in exclusionary discipline: The Role of School Policy. *Urban Education, 42*(6), 536–559. Retrieved from http://sagepub.com

Gerber, M. M. (2005). Teachers are still the test: Limitations of response to instruction strategies for identifying children with learning disabilities. *Journal of Learning Disabilities, 38*(6), 516–524.

Gregory, A., Skiba, R. J., & Noguera, P. A. (2010). The achievement gap and the discipline gap: Two sides of the same coin? *Educational Researcher, 39*(1), 59–68. Retrieved from http://sagepub.com

Individuals with Disabilities Education Act (IDEA), 20 U.S.C. §1400 (2004).

Krezmlen, M. P., Leone, P. E., & Achilles, G. M. (2006). Suspension, race, and disability: Analysis of statewide practices and reporting. *Journal of Emotional & Behavioral Disorders, 14*(4), 217–226. https://doi.org/10.1177/10634266060140040501

National Center for Educational Statistics (NCES). (2021). Students with disabilities. Retrieved September 14, 2021 from https://nces.ed.gov/programs/coe/indicator/cgg

Oliver, R. M., & Reschly, D. J. (2010). Special education teacher preparation in classroom management: Implications for students with emotional and behavioral disorders. *Behavioral Disorders, 35*(3), 188–199.

Oshima, K. M. M., Huang, J., Jonson-Reid, M., & Drake, B. (2010). Children with disabilities in poor households: Association with juvenile and adult offending. *Social Work Research, 34*(2), 102–113.

Packman, J., & Bratton, S. C. (2003). A school-based group play/activity therapy intervention with learning disabled preadolescents exhibiting behavior problems. *International Journal of Play Therapy, 12*(2), 7–29. https://doi.org/10.1037/h0088876

Quinn, M. M., Rutherford, R. B., Leone, P. E., Osher, D. M., & Poirier, J. M. (2005). Youth with disabilities in juvenile corrections: A national survey. *Exceptional Children, 71*(3), 339–345. https://doi.org/10.1177/001440290507100308

Simonsen, B., Fairbanks, S., Briesch, A., Myers, D., & Sugai, G. (2008). Evidence-based practices in classroom management: Considerations for research to practice. *Education & Treatment of Children, 31*(3), 351–380. https://doi.org/10.1353/etc.0.0007

Skiba, R. J., Peterson, R. L., & Williams, T. (1997). Office referrals and suspension: Disciplinary intervention in middle school. *Education & Treatment of Children, 20*(3), 295.

Slaughter, E. (2018). Juvenile incarceration and justice in the United States. *American Jails, 32*(3), 8.

Vincent, C. G., Sprague, J. R., & Tobin, T. J. (2012). Empirical study of patterns in disciplinary exclusions of students with learning disabilities by grade, ethnicity, race, and gender in a response to intervention framework. *Insights on Learning Disabilities, 9*(1), 69–91.

Whitford, D. K. (2017). School discipline disproportionality: American Indian students in special education. *Urban Review: Issues and Ideas in Public Education, 49*(5), 693–706. Retrieved from http://www.springerlink.com

An Overview of the History of Special Education

Chapter 2 provides an overview of the history of special education in the United States of America (US). Chapter 2 begins with the story of Hellen Keller as a way of illustrating the fact that before special education legislation in 1975 was passed, very few individuals with disabilities went to school, and many were from households with the money to send them to private schools. The chapter continues with Elizabeth Farrell, the first special education teacher in the US, who established the ungraded classroom. The chapter goes on to discuss the thorny issue of institutionalization of individuals with disabilities and segregated classrooms or schools for individuals with disabilities. The second part of Chapter 2 emphasizes the history of parent advocacy for children with disabilities and highlights major cases that have strengthened the rights of parents or guardians of children with disabilities. This includes an explanation of how these cases paved the way for the Individuals with Disabilities Education Improvement Act (IDEA, 2004), the federal special education law which governs the education and treatment of students with disabilities in the US. Chapter 2 closes with a discussion of the major revisions of the IDEA that have strengthened the rights of students with disabilities and increased school accountability in providing quality and research-based educational services.

All Future Educators
Students with disabilities have not always had a right to public education. Parental involvement and advocacy have facilitated a change in the educational rights of children.

Elementary General Education
Interventions during early elementary education is recognized to help prevent future learning difficulties. Part of early intervention requires teachers to collaborate with families about the educational needs of their child.

Secondary General Education
Students with disabilities must be provided access to a general education curriculum to help prepare them for college-level academic success. This requires general education teachers to work with special educators in developing appropriate instruction and goals.

Special Education
Students with disabilities are less likely to graduate from high school. To address this concern, a greater emphasis has been placed on transition services to help prepare students for their postsecondary life based on student interest and strengths.

Undergraduates Interested in Disability Laws
The law is not an unbending and unrelenting entity. Education laws have changed over time in response to both parent advocacy and scientific research.

In this chapter, readers will:

- Learn the history of special education from 1975 to the present.
- Understand the role parents have played in establishing advocacy groups for children with disabilities.
- Understand the impact and unique nature of special education case law in the US.
- Learn how IDEA has changed over time to better support students with disabilities in public schools.

After reading this chapter, readers will be able to:

- Chronicle important years in case law and major revisions to the IDEA that influenced the development of special education from 1975 to the present.
- Discuss the aspects of special education case law that promote parental involvement.

History of Special Education in the United States

The year 1975 was a turning point in the history of special education in the US. While some states did provide special education to students with disabilities, students who lived in states without special education services did not attend school. There were many cases and small bits of legislation which paved the way for this watershed year, but the single most important piece of federal legislation, then known as the Education for All Handicapped Children Act, was passed in 1975. In 1990, the Education for All Handicapped Children Act was renamed as the Individuals with Disabilities Education Act (IDEA). The IDEA was again amended in 2004, and presently the complete name of the federal special education law is the Individuals with Disabilities Education Improvement Act, which continues to be referred to as IDEA.

Prior to 1975, children with disabilities were commonly excluded from public education (Spaulding & Pratt, 2015). Children who were educated in schools were there because of the benevolence of school administrators. Most children with disabilities who went to school had parents who could afford to pay for private teachers or schools. The story of Helen Keller illustrates how wealthy families educated a child with a disability. Helen, one of several children of a wealthy family, lost her vision and hearing around the age of 19 months after an illness speculated to be meningitis or rubella, though it is not known which with certainty. In 1887, when Helen was 7 years old, Anne Sullivan was hired to live with the Keller family to teach Helen in her home. Sullivan, being blind herself, taught Helen to communicate, read, and write (Edwards, 2002). Under Sullivan's tutelage, Helen attended the Perkins School for the Blind in 1888, with her teacher Ms. Sullivan accompanying her to school. In 1894, the two moved to New York to allow Helen to attend the Wright-Humason School for the Deaf. Helen later enrolled in Radcliffe College of Harvard University and graduated with a Bachelor of Arts degree in 1904, becoming the first student ever who was both deaf and blind to graduate from Harvard University. Sullivan's relationship with Helen lasted over 50 years and evolved from teacher to governess, and eventually to companion. All the while, Helen's family paid to allow Helen to have these educational experiences.

The opportunities for education and travel that Helen enjoyed while growing up were not available to all individuals with disabilities who were Helen's contemporaries. Most people with disabilities who did not have similar parental engagement and financial resources to hire private tutors or to pay tuition to attend private schools stayed at home with their families or were sent to live in institutions. For most individuals with disabilities, if they picked up a trade, it was learned from their parents or a family member, informally. Prior to 1975, individuals with disabilities relied wholly on the financial support of their families to pay for their educations. Furthermore, prior to 1975, individuals with disabilities were expected to find a way to circumvent their disabilities themselves if they were in any program outside of their home (i.e., Helen brought her tutors to school; the school did not provide assistance). Individuals who lacked money to pay for school were excluded from education.

The First Special Education Teacher

Elizabeth Farrell was the first special education teacher in the US. She started her career as a teacher at Public School #1 in New York City after graduating from college in 1895 (Kode, 2001). According to Kode (2001), Ms. Farrell was assigned to teach a class of "misfit" boys of different ages in 1899. Notably, Ms. Farrell was not trained as a special education teacher when she was given the responsibility to teach the ungraded class. According to Hendrick and MacMillan (2017), in the early stages of special education, teachers who taught students with disabilities did not receive any specialized training. Teachers received some additional pay for teaching in ungraded classrooms, but that was all. The original ungraded classrooms in New York's school system were reported to have been designed for students suspected of having intellectual disabilities or physical disabilities (Hendrick & MacMillan, 2017). Interestingly, however, one wonders why the group of boys assigned to Ms. Farrell to teach were referred to as "misfits." Were these children considered misfits because they did not fit the learning pattern of the rest of the students? Were these students referred to as misfits because they were disruptive in the classroom and exhibited inappropriate classroom behavior? Ms. Farrell's opinion, according to Hendrick and MacMillan (2017), was that the children she taught were in her class because of truancy and school disciplinary challenges they posed to the regular classes.

Ungraded classrooms were small, having between 12 to 20 students. The curriculum in the ungraded classroom that Ms. Farrell developed was student-centered and interactive. Ms. Farrell used tin cans, puzzles, paints and brushes, music, and dance to engage her students when she taught. She served her students food and invited parents to partake in lunches in her classroom with their children and Ms. Farrell's other students. In the ungraded classroom, teachers were expected to engage the student based on his or her interests. In addition, the ungraded classroom Ms. Farrell provided included work benches, running water to clean students, and a focus on practical skills. The ungraded classroom proved to be highly popular among parents and positive in the lives of students. Ms. Farrell conducted an evaluation of the success of the ungraded classrooms and found that many of the students placed in an ungraded classroom continued to attend school instead of dropping out. In fact, many of the students who completed the ungraded classroom curriculum were later employed (Hendrick & MacMillan, 2017).

Placement decisions for an ungraded classroom were conducted by the school principal who referred the student after a physical examination by a physician (Hendrick & MacMillan, 2017). In

1904, Martin Barr published a classification system in which he divided students with intellectual disabilities into five subcategories, one of them being described as "backward or mentally feeble"—students in this subcategory were deemed capable to benefit from general education curriculum since their mental capacity was normal, but they learned more slowly (Barr, 1904). Although intelligence testing had nothing to do with the development of special education classes, their use after the tests were introduced into the schooling system in New York in the 1920s took on a life of its own. From the start of their use, intelligence tests over-identified children of immigrant households. Nonetheless, in the early days of special education (or ungraded classrooms), parents did not speak out against the use of intelligence tests because the alternative for their children was to have them at home without access to any education if they could not afford to pay for their children's education.

Institutionalization Versus Deinstitutionalization

The institutionalization of individuals with disabilities is a highly debated practice questioned from its early use to the present (National Council on Disability, 2019). In the past, more people with disabilities lived in institutions compared to current times. **Institutionalization** occurred if families could not, or would not, keep the child with a disability at home. These children lived in segregated facilities, or institutions, away from their families and the general society. However, institutionalization in and of itself is neither good nor bad for people with disabilities. The medical model presumes that people with disabilities are sick and in need of medical assistance and must be cared for by medical professionals. In instances where the individual is uncared for at home, an institution provides shelter and basic necessities to the individual. However, this is not always the case, and individuals in institutions can be treated inhumanely (National Council on Disability, 2019). Institutions like the New York State Lunatic Asylum used chains, caged beds, and straitjackets were used to restrain patients with mental illnesses and are the focus of rightful criticism against the institutionalization of people with disabilities.

Critics of institutionalization argue that people with disabilities have the right to remain in their homes instead of being removed from society and locked away from their families and communities. The critics argue that institutionalization treats people with disabilities in a paternalistic manner because they are deprived of their freedom and of the right to actively exercise self-determination in their daily lives (National Council on Disability, 2019). Critics of institutionalization point to the poor treatment and dire conditions in which many people with disabilities were kept. On the other hand, while promoting self-determination among individuals with disabilities of all levels should be the ultimate goal, some individuals with significant disabilities require intensive support.

If the individual does not have the family or community support to make safe choices for living in their daily lives, living in an institution can be safer than living outside an institution, alone and without any support. Therefore, some people with disabilities do benefit from living in the care of professionals who are trained in the care of individuals with disabilities. Proponents of institutionalization argue that having institutions as one of many choices where people with disabilities can receive care is the most important argument for having a continuum of services. Proponents of having the option of caring for some people with disabilities in an institution when it is necessary argue that removing the option of being in an institution altogether, and without having community-based care in place, makes people with disabilities more vulnerable rather than independent.

Scholars and advocates of having a continuum of placement services believe that some individuals with disabilities require assistance to meet their daily needs (Ochoa, 2011). They point to the era of **deinstitutionalization** that started with benign intentions in the 1960s with President John F. Kennedy signing the Community Mental Health Act as the beginning of the end of publicly funded services for people with disabilities who were institutionalized. By the Reagan presidential era of the 1980s, many people with disabilities who were previously institutionalized found themselves destitute in the streets or in correctional facilities, trading one institution for another. As such, the level of care and independence should ideally be based on the individual needs of the person.

Full Inclusion Versus Partial Inclusion

As of the early 1970s, US schools only educated one in five children with disabilities, and many states had laws that excluded certain students with disabilities, such as those with significant visual and hearing impairments, those with emotional disabilities, and those with intellectual disabilities (U.S. Department of Education, 2022). However, currently less than 1% of students with disabilities are provided with services in their homes (homebound services) or in residential settings, like hospitals or correctional institution settings (National Center for Educational Statistics [NCES], 2021).

As discussed, it was not until the passage of the first special education law in 1975 that special education became a guarantee for students with disabilities. Unfortunately, even though special education was conceptualized as a benefit to support students with disabilities (Ochoa, 2011), the argument against special education has been associated with the argument against institutionalization. Settings like resource rooms, self-contained classrooms, and special day schools are often thought about as equivalent to the practice of segregating students from their non-disabled peers. Thus, special education, in the minds of many, is another form of institutionalization.

IDEA states that public schools are required to educate students with disabilities in the general education setting to the fullest extent possible, based solely on the needs of the student and the severity of their disability (IDEA, §1412, 2004). This statement in the IDEA has resulted in the minds of many people a preference for keeping students with disabilities in the general education classroom at all costs. Some critics of special education believe that settings outside of the general education classroom are outright discriminatory against students with disabilities and advocate for **full inclusion**. The full inclusion movement indicates that every student with a disability in need of special education must receive all services in the general education classroom. In practice, that means that under no circumstance should a student with a disability be removed from the general education classroom during any portion of the day. There is no legal support for full inclusion. In fact, full inclusion as an only option for all students with disabilities is a violation of the IDEA.

> *Schools are required to educate students with disabilities in the general education setting to the fullest extent possible, based solely on the needs of the student and the severity of their disability.*

IDEA states that the individual needs of the student must be taken into account when determining placement. The IDEA requires a continuum of special education services in schools that range from full inclusion in general education classes to separate classrooms designed to meet the more intensive needs of students with disabilities. As such, if a student needs to be in a resource room for part of the time to get special education like reading support or speech support, the IDEA allows for that student to spend that instructional time outside of the general education classroom. **Partial inclusion** is a more measured approach to the provision of special education because it allows for instances in which students need to spend some instructional time outside of the general education classroom. While full inclusion may sound appealing, when it is applied to all students with disabilities indiscriminately of their individual needs, it is a denial of their rights to the individualized instruction the IDEA offers them. To be sure, students should receive special education services in the general education classroom to the maximum extent possible. However, to safeguard their rights to the least restrictive environment (LRE) provision of the IDEA, they must be in a setting that does not restrict their learning. Sometimes, the LRE for students with disabilities may be a resource room, a special education classroom, or a special education day school.

Groundbreaking Special Education Cases

The civil rights movement of the 1960s was the impetus for the shift from exclusion to inclusion of individuals with disabilities into mainstream society. The disabilities movement was an extension of the larger societal civil rights era and argued that excluding individuals with disabilities from school was a practice as unjust as separating Black people from the general society.

Litigation has been an unfortunate yet instrumental tool in the improvement of the lives of individuals with disabilities in the US (Ochoa, 2011). In this section, four groundbreaking cases which paved the way for the watershed special education legislation in the US are discussed. As a group, these cases served to level the playing field for individuals with disabilities who do not have financial resources such as those which Helen Keller's family had, to pay for the education of their children with disabilities.

> *Litigation has been an unfortunate yet instrumental tool in the improvement of the lives of individuals with disabilities.*

The ***Pennsylvania Association for Retarded People (PARC) v. Commonwealth of Pennsylvania*** was the first time a state-level law was judged to be unfair and unconstitutional against individuals with intellectual disabilities. In the *PARC* case, 13 families sued the state of Pennsylvania because schools were legally allowed to turn away students with intellectual and developmental disabilities who could not function at grade level or could not function in the general classroom instruction. The 1972 judgment sided with the families and upheld their viewpoint that schooling was beneficial to individuals with intellectual impairments, even if such students did not reach the same academic levels as other students. The judgment said that some learning was better than no learning and that, in the end, being in school benefited individuals with intellectual disabilities. The most significant aspect of the *PARC* case was that schools could no longer have a legal mechanism to deny access to public education to students with intellectual disabilities. In other words, schools in Pennsylvania could no longer turn away students with intellectual disabilities (Ochoa, 2011).

Mills v. Board of Education of the District of Columbia was similar to *PARC*, except that the *Mills* case was heard at the US Supreme Court level. The Mills case was on behalf of students with different disabilities. In 1972, the parents of seven children in the District of Columbia filed a class action suit on behalf of children with hyperactive disorder (now referred to as attention deficit hyperactivity disorder), slight brain damage, epilepsy, and mental retardation (now referred to as intellectual disabilities). Parents argued that their children were being denied appropriate educational services compared to the education other students were receiving. Some of these children were put on a waiting list to receive a grant or award to attend a private school, but no awards were ever issued (Ochoa, 2011). Thus, the parents argued they could not afford to pay for the educational programs their children needed. The US Supreme Court ruled that schools could not use the pretext of financial burden to exclude students with disabilities from having access to education. The court ordered the schools to reallocate their funding so as not to exclude students with disabilities from having a free public education. Prior to the *PARC* case and the *Mills* case rulings, schools could turn away students with disabilities or could say they did not have money to pay for programs for students with disabilities. The *PARC* and *Mills* cases proved instrumental in securing the right to public education at public expense for students with disabilities (Lengyel & Van Bergeijk, 2021).

The ***Board of Education of the Hendrick Hudson Central School District v. Rowley*** case from 1982 is significant in the history of special education because it was the first time the US Supreme Court interpreted the meaning of free appropriate public education (FAPE, Rowley, 2008). Amy Rowley was a student with hearing impairments with excellent lip-reading skills. When Amy entered kindergarten, she was provided adaptive technology as part of her special education programming. In addition, some school administrators took a sign language course to be able to communicate with Amy's parents who were also hearing impaired. Amy finished her kindergarten year successfully. At the start of first grade, Amy's parents were supportive of most of what the school committee responsible for preparing Amy's educational programming recommended for their daughter. The only exception was that the parents requested a qualified sign language interpreter in all of Amy's academic classes. After careful consideration, the school administrators disagreed with Amy's parents, who in turn sought a hearing officer to hear their complaint. After hearing evidence from both sides, the ruling from the hearing officer was in favor of the school. The hearing officer reasoned that because Amy was achieving academically and socially without such interpreter, the parents' request was justifiably denied.

When the *Rowley* case reached the US Supreme Court and the court rendered its decision, it said that schools were not obligated to ensure maximum learning benefit for any student with a disability.

However, the Supreme Court did stipulate that schools must provide compelling evidence that they followed appropriate procedures to provide evidence that a student's individual education program was written in such a way as to provide meaningful educational benefit to students with disabilities. Parents and schools must work collaboratively to communicate with one another to develop appropriate goals for students with disabilities and to develop a plan to work toward those goals. In sum, the parents cannot force schools to do what is beyond their reach, but in turn, schools must listen to the concerns of parents when it comes to the education of their children with disabilities.

Endrew F. v. Douglas County School District reached a US Supreme Court–level ruling in 2017. The case involved Endrew, a student with autism, who failed to reach his educational programming goals in public school from kindergarten to 4th grade (Turnbull et al., 2018). Under the belief that the school was not providing appropriate goals for Endrew, his parents transferred him to a private school, where he reached academic, social, and behavioral goals. The disagreement between Endrew's parents and the school was about a challenging curriculum. The school argued that they were required only to provide minimal educational benefit to Endrew. On the other hand, Endrew's parents believed that he was entitled to a more rigorous academic program. The Supreme Court said that children with disabilities are, in fact, entitled to more than just the minimum benefit. In the *Endrew* case, the US Supreme Court said that schools must offer students with disabilities an educational program that is "reasonably calculated to enable a child to make progress appropriate in light of the child's circumstances." Legal scholars have interpreted the court's ruling in the *Endrew* case to mean that schools' responsibility is to hold higher expectations for students with disabilities, beyond the bare minimum. Therefore, schools must go from mere access to inclusion and education to accountability for the academic achievement of students with disabilities.

Major Revisions of IDEA

The IDEA is a living document which changes over time and across presidential administrations. In this section, we will discuss some of the main topics of the revisions that occurred in 1997, 2004, and 2017 and their implications for students with disabilities.

1997: Disciplining Students with Disability and Manifestation Determination. Prior to the 1997 revision of the IDEA, the only provision that addressed school discipline and students with disabilities stated that students with disabilities could be removed from the general education environment and placed in an alternative education placement for up to 45 days if the student brought a gun to the school or to a school function. The following revisions, or amendments, were incorporated into the IDEA in 1997 (United States Department of Education [U.S. DOE], 1999):

- Schools could remove a child for up to 10 school days at a time for any violation of school rules as long as there was not a pattern of removals.
- A child with a disability could not be long-term suspended or expelled from school for behavior that was a manifestation of his or her disability.
- Services must continue for children with disabilities who are suspended or expelled from school.

- Expanded the authority of school personnel regarding the removal of a child who brings a gun to school, to also apply to all dangerous weapons and to the knowing possession of illegal drugs or the sale or solicitation or the sale of controlled substances.
- Added a new ability of schools to request a hearing officer to remove a child for up to 45 days if keeping the child in his or her current placement is substantially likely to result in injury to the child or to others.

The purpose of the 1997 revision was to provide students with disabilities protection from being removed from schools due to the nature, or manifestation of, their disability. If a student is removed from school for 10 days consecutively or 10 days based on separate acts, schools are not required to provide services during those 10 days. However, the school should examine their current services and determine if additional provisions or evaluation is warranted to determine whether the student would benefit from additional services to address problematic behavior.

2004: High-Stakes Testing and Alignment with No Child Left Behind (NCLB). In 2001, under President George W. Bush, the No Child Left Behind (NCLB) Act was signed into law. The purpose of NCLB was to ensure that children receive a high-quality education and to put in provisions that would hold schools and districts accountable (U.S. DOE, 2007). Below are the primary topics addressed in the NCLB (2001):

- Support learning in the early years to prevent future learning difficulties.
- Provide more information for parents about student progress through state assessment or testing, which are aligned with state grade level standards.
- Alert parents or guardians to important information regarding their child's school.
- Give families school choice, allowing parents to move students to a higher-performing school or receive supplemental educational services.
- Improve teaching and learning by providing information to teachers and administrators.
- Provide more resources to and allow more flexibility in the use of federal funds in an effort to improve education of disadvantaged students, turn around low-performing schools, improve teacher quality, and increase school choice; and
- Focus on educational programs and practices that are supported through rigorous scientific research.

However, the annual state testing that is required by the NCLB only provides a snapshot of student performance on grade level standards and is not an accurate measure of student growth or improvement. Allbritten et al. (2004) posit that the pretest and posttest scores that measure growth, which is a common method of monitoring IEP goals, may be a more appropriate measure of school and district performance. Allbritten et al. also criticize the lack of organization and coordination between policy makers to align the 2001 NCLB with the 1997 IDEA.

In 2004, the revisions to IDEA were signed into law. The following regulations were introduced to align the IDEA with the NCLB:

- Early intervening services for children not currently identified as needing special education but who need additional academic and behavioral support to succeed in a general education environment.
- Greater accountability and improved educational outcomes.
- Raised standards for instructors who teach special education classes.

For students currently identified with special education disabilities, the 2004 revisions also include the development of appropriate accommodations and alternative assessments that are valid and reliable for assessing the performance of students with disabilities, as well as technical assistance and direct services to children with disabilities in schools or districts that have been identified for improvement due to the assessment results of students with disabilities. Additionally, these funds can be used for professional development focused on improving educational instruction for both special education and general education teachers.

2015: Every Student Succeeds Act (ESSA) and Students with Disabilities. In 2015, under President Barack Obama, the Every Student Succeeds Act (ESSA) was signed into law. The purpose of the ESSA was to revise the NCLB and address the educational inequities that face the nation's most vulnerable and high-needs children. Below are the highlights of the changes made in the 2015 ESSA:

- Requires that all students be taught to high academic standards which can prepare them to succeed in college and careers.
- Ensures that vital information is provided to educators, families, students, and communities through annual statewide assessments that measure students' progress toward those high standards.
- Helps to support and grow local innovations, including evidence-based and place-based interventions developed by local leaders and educators.
- Sustains and expands increasing access to high-quality preschool.
- Maintains an expectation that there will be accountability and action to effect positive change in our lowest-performing schools, where groups of students are not making progress and where graduation rates are low over extended periods of time.

In 2017, revisions to the IDEA were signed into law. The changes made to the IDEA were mostly technical changes, designed to align the language used in the ESSA and to update any provisions outlined in the ESSA that directly related to students with disabilities, such as providing specific guidance in supporting students in postsecondary transition (college and careers). Tomasello & Brand (2018) reported that students with disabilities were: less likely to graduate from high school (65%) compared to their non-disabled peers (83%); were less likely to obtain a bachelor's level or high level degree (14%) compared to their non-disabled peers (33%); were less likely to be employed as adults (35%) compared to their non-disabled peers (78%); and earned on average of $5,000–$11,000 less that their non-disabled peers. The ESSA and IDEA strategies to address support students with disabilities in college and career readiness are as follows (Tomasello & Brand, 2018):

- High expectations and access to the general education curriculum designed to prepare students to earn a high school diploma and prepare them for college-level academic expectations.
- College and career advising and transition planning to inform students of postsecondary opportunities, including college and careers.

- Career pathways that connect what is learned inside the classroom to postsecondary college and career choice.
- Dual and concurrent enrollment that allows high school students access to college-level coursework and time on a college campus.
- Personalized and competency-based learning that focuses on the interest, needs, and skills of the student and which allows a student to work at their own pace.

The changes and updates from 1997 to 2017 were designed to reflect the changing needs and understanding of students with disabilities. The 1997 changes primarily focus on providing students with disability safeguards that prevent schools from removing students for reasons directly related to their disability, special education services, or related services. It is designed to hold schools accountable for student behavior and increase the likelihood that students with disabilities will remain in the general education setting to improve educational outcomes. In 2004, there was a greater focus on school accountability. The changes made in the NCLB (2001) allowed for more flexibility in the use of federal resources to providing early academic and behavioral interventions for students who are at-risk, in an effort to prevent the need for special education. The ESSA of 2015 and subsequent 2017 revisions of the IDEA move beyond K–12 schools in general and focus its efforts on supporting students with the greatest needs, as well as putting into place policies that will ensure that schools focus on postsecondary transition in an effort to address the post-secondary education, career, and wage gaps that exist between students with disabilities and their non-disabled counterparts. As time goes on, federal education laws and IDEA will continue to evolve to reflect the policies of the current administration and the needs of the most vulnerable and high-risk students, including those with disabilities.

Summary

Historically, individuals with disabilities were separated from their non-disabled peers and were often placed in institutions. Even when education became compulsory, individuals with disabilities were often denied entry to public schools or were placed in separate classrooms than their non-disabled counterparts. Special education has changed over time through parental advocacy for children with disabilities. In schools today, the debate continues between what is known as full inclusion versus partial inclusion or self-contained classrooms. In Chapter 3, we will discuss the three main federal special education laws and provide more detailed information on the continuum of care and services available for students with disabilities. We will go into greater detail about student needs and characteristics in Chapter 4.

Test Your Knowledge

1. What familial factors explain Helen Keller's success in her personal and professional life?
2. Compared to Helen Keller's circumstances, what might explain why her contemporaries with similar impairments might not have achieved similar levels of success?
3. Who is Elizabeth Farrell, and what is her contribution to the field of special education and special education teacher preparation?

4. Summarize the four major cases (*PARC*, *Mills*, *Rowley*, & *Endrew*) discussed in the chapter and state what benefits they established for students with disabilities.
5. Summarize the three major revisions of the IDEA (1997, 2004, 2017) and state what benefits they established for students with disabilities.

Apply Your Knowledge

Ask

Ask yourself the following question to help guide your reading.

- What are the benefits and drawbacks to institutionalization, self-contained classrooms, and full inclusion?

Read
Read the following sections.

- Institutionalization Versus Deinstitutionalization (p. 12)
- Self-Contained Versus Inclusion (p. 13)
- Historical and Current Groundbreaking Special Education Cases (p. 14)

Tell
Tell your response.

- Do all students with disabilities benefit from full inclusion? Using what you have read and any professional or personal experience you have, explain your response.

References

Barr, M. W. (1904). Classification of mental defectives. *Journal of Psychoasthetics, 9*, 20–38.

Edwards, R.A.R. (2002). Seeing and hearing in a deaf-blind world: Laura Bridgman's view. Essay. *Journal of the Historical Society, 2*(3/4), 337–354.

Kode, K. (2001). Guarding the sacred fires: Elizabeth E. Farrell's contributions to the creation of special education in New York City. *Dissertations (1962–2010). Access via Proquest Digital Dissertations.* AAI3049933. https://epublications.marquette.edu/dissertations/AAI3049933

Hendrick, I. G., & MacMillan, D. L. (2017). Selecting children for special education in New York City: William Maxwell, Elizabeth Farrell, and the development of ungraded classes, 1900–1920. *The Journal of Special Education, 22*(4), 395–417.

Individuals with Disabilities Education Improvement Act of 2004, 20 U.S.C. §1412 (IDEA, 2004), Pub. L. No. 108-446, 118 Stat. 2652.

Lengyel, S. L., & Van Bergeijk, E. (2021). A brief history of special education: Milestones in the first 50 years. *Exceptional Parent, 51*(7), 37–40.

National Center for Education Statistics (NCES). (2021). *Digest of education statistics, 2019* (NCES 2021-009), Chapter 2. https://nces.ed.gov/pubs2021/2021009.pdf

National Council on Disability (May 24, 2019). Preserving our freedom: Ending institutionalization of people with disabilities during and after disasters. Washington, DC. www.ncd.gov

Ochoa, T. A. (2011). Bilingual special education. In C. J. Ovando and M. C. Combs (Eds.), *Bilingual and ESL classrooms* (5th ed., pp. 367–395). McGraw Hill.

Rowley, A. J. (2008). Rowley revisited: A personal narrative. *Journal of Law & Education, 37*(3), 311–328.

Spaulding, L. S., & Pratt, S. M. (2015). A review analysis of the history of special education and disability advocacy in the United States. *American Educational History Journal, 42*(1), 91–109.

Tomasello, J., & Brand, B. (2018). *How ESSA and IDEA can support college and career readiness for students with disabilities: Considerations for states.* College & Career Readiness & Success. https://files.eric.ed.gov/fulltext/ED586419.pdf

Turnbull, H. R., Turnbull, A. P., & Cooper, D. H. (2018). The Supreme Court, Endrew, and the appropriate education of students with disabilities. *Exceptional Children, 84*(2), 124–140. https://doi-org.proxyiub.uits.iu.edu/10.1177/0014402917734150

U.S. Department of Education. (March 18, 2022). *A History of the Individuals with Disabilities Education Act.* U.S. Department of Education, Individuals with Disabilities Act. https://sites.ed.gov/idea/IDEA-History

Federal Disability Laws

Chapter 3 discusses the three federal disability laws in the United States of America (US): the Americans with Disabilities Act Amendments Act (ADAAA), Section 504 of the Rehabilitation Act (Section 504), and the Individuals with Disabilities Education Improvement Act (IDEA). Emphasis is placed on the provisions of the IDEA. Among the three laws discussed in this chapter, the IDEA is the only special education law. Section 504 and ADAAA are antidiscrimination laws. The chapter begins by describing each disability law and its purpose, noting similarities and differences between the three at the end of the chapter.

In this chapter, readers will:

- Learn the three most relevant federal disability laws.
- Develop an understanding of the legal provisions, or benefits, that the IDEA offers to students with disabilities.

Gain insight on the evolving nature of the three disability laws and the importance of following changes to ensure that students' and families' rights are consistent with the letter and spirit of each disability law.

After reading this chapter, readers will be able to:

- Identify the similarities and differences between the three disability laws.
- Identify where each disability law applies.

All Future Educators
Federal disability laws are designed to protect all students with disabilities; most students with disabilities are educated in general education classrooms.

Elementary General Education
General education teachers are often the primary contact for most families. Nurturing the relationships between school and family is essential as parental involvement in student learning is instrumental for long-term positive outcomes.

Secondary General Education
General education teachers can collaborate with special education teachers and students to help design and implement effective transition goals and services.

Special Education
Special education teachers are responsible for managing the IEPs for students with disabilities. This includes monitoring discipline decisions to ensure students' rights to appropriate education in the least restrictive setting are not violated.

Undergraduates Interested in Disability Laws
Removing students with disabilities from school through disciplinary decisions not only increases their risk of incarceration (Chapter 1), but also violates their civil rights (ADAA & Section 504) and their rights to appropriate education in the least restrictive setting under the IDEA.

- Identify and discuss the main provisions of the IDEA.
- Discuss the role and responsibilities educators play in the education of students with disabilities.
- Discuss how school closures and remote learning in response to the COVID-19 global pandemic may have impacted access to the general education curriculum for students with disabilities.

Americans with Disabilities Act Amendments Act

The **Americans with Disabilities Act Amendments Act (ADAAA)** is a federal civil rights law that prohibits discrimination against all individuals with disabilities. Congress amended the definition of disability in the law so it would be "construed broadly." In doing so, the ADAAA of 2018 increased the list of major life activities to include, for example, concentration, eating, neurological issues, and bowel functions. It also explained that "ameliorative effects of mitigating measures," such as medication, prosthetic limbs, hearing aids, and use of technology, should not be considered when determining whether an impairment substantially limits a major life activity (ADAAA, 2018). The ADAAA mandates elementary, secondary, and higher postsecondary schools to make reasonable accommodations to students who are considered as having a disability. Of note, the ADAAA extends outside of federally funded programs and institutions into all areas of public life, including all public and private institutions that are accessible to the public. The ADAAA applies also to places of employment.

The Purpose of the ADAAA

The purpose of the ADAAA is to:

- Provide a clear and comprehensive national mandate for the elimination of discrimination against individuals with disabilities;
- Provide clear, strong, consistent, enforceable standards addressing discrimination against individuals with disabilities;
- Ensure that the federal government plays a central role in enforcing the standards established on behalf of individuals with disabilities;
- To invoke the sweep of congressional authority (the power to enact federal laws) to address the major areas of discrimination faced day-to-day by people with disabilities.

The ADAAA in Public Schools

In public school settings, the ADAAA focuses on accessibility to the environment, such as providing wheelchair ramps and accessible bathrooms, as well as providing aids and services like providing braille documents for individuals with visual impairments. The ADAAA does not require schools to provide free and appropriate public education (FAPE). As such, the ADAAA is more limited in its daily impact on the education of elementary and secondary level students compared to Section 504 of the Rehabilitation Act. The ADAAA does not have any educational provisions to provide accommodations to students in schools. However, legal experts have noted that the latest reauthorization of the ADAAA is likely to require more substantive accommodations to students in higher education than it had previously.

Accommodations provided in the ADAAA (U.S. DOE OCR, 2020a) include:

- Reasonable changes in policies, practices, and procedures that are aimed to avoid discrimination based on disability;
- Aids and services for individuals with hearing or vision impairments to provide an equal opportunity to participate in, or benefit from, services;
- Removing physical barriers or providing alternative methods to access environments or services (e.g., buildings, bathrooms, transportation) available to people without disabilities. As such, the ADAAA encourages entities to alter existing environments to be more accessible to individuals with disabilities if buildings or structures were constructed before 1990. New construction of buildings must ensure that they provide access to individuals with disabilities.

In sum, ADAAA protects individuals with disabilities against discrimination based on their disability, but does not provide any type of funding or services.

Section 504 of Rehabilitation Act of 1973

The Purpose of Section 504

Section 504 of the Rehabilitation Act of 1973 (Section 504) is a civil rights law. Section 504 protects individuals with disabilities from being subjected to discrimination under or exclusion from any program or activity receiving federal financial assistance or conducted by any government agency. This includes local educational agencies (LEA), such as schools. Section 504 applies to elementary, secondary, and postsecondary entities, such as colleges, state and local governments, hospital and mental health organizations, and private organizations which receive federal financial assistance.

Section 504 protects all qualified individuals with disabilities. *Disability* is defined as an impairment (mental or physical) that limits major life activities, which includes impairments that impact the ability to care for oneself, breathe, work, and learn. Section 504 provides some examples of areas that may be included as disabilities (U.S. Department of Health and Human Services [DHHS], 2006), such as acquired immunodeficiency syndrome (AIDS), alcoholism and drug addiction, visual and hearing impairments, diabetes, heart disease, and mental illness. To be considered as an individual with a disability under Section 504, individuals must meet eligibility requirements or criteria, according to medical and mental health diagnoses. Protections in Section 504 aim to prevent discrimination against individuals with disabilities by preventing the following actions from federally funded programs or organizations (U.S. DHHS, 2006):

- Denying qualified individuals the opportunity to participate in or benefit from federally funded programs, services, or other benefits;
- Denying access to programs, services, benefits, or opportunities to participate as a result of physical barriers;
- Denying employment opportunities, including hiring, promotion, training, and fringe benefits, for which they are otherwise entitled to receive or qualified to hold.

Section 504 in Public Schools

Section 504 is the first comprehensive disability law to protect and provide benefits to students with disabilities in public schools. Students at all levels of education (elementary, secondary, and higher education) are protected against discrimination under Section 504. Notably, Section 504 also protects parents with disabilities, and it mandates schools to provide the same level of access to parents with disabilities that schools provide for all parents to be able to participate in the educational process (Hulett, 2009). Section 504 mandates schools to provide individualized plans to ensure that students with disabilities have a free and appropriate public education (FAPE). Under Section 504, FAPE includes general education, special education, and related services to meet students' specific needs (U.S. Department of Education Office of Civil Rights [U.S. DOE OCR], 2020b). Related services include academic, social-emotional, and behavioral supports. Section 504 requires schools to provide specific accommodations to students under its broad definition of disability. The Office of Civil Rights within the Department of Education ensures that schools comply with Section 504 requirements.

504 Plans

Schools and school districts are required to provide accommodations to students with disabilities under Section 504 (U.S. DOE OCR, 2020b). Specific accommodations and modifications are known as 504 Plans within Section 504 of the Rehabilitation Act. By definition, an **accommodation** changes *how* the student learns or accesses the educational material. For example, Zirkel et al. (2012) reported that 15% of students with food allergies had a reaction in school. Allergic reactions can vary from minor to severe and can potentially be life threatening. A 504 plan would provide accommodations to the environment to prevent exposure to allergens, how to intervene if exposure has occurred, and would also prevent students from being penalized academically due to the medical condition. Below are samples of accommodations in 504 plans (McGlynn & Kelly, 2019). In other cases, such as for students with attention deficit hyperactivity disorder, a 504 plan may provide testing in small groups or preferential seating away from distractions to address inattention related to the disorder. Table 3.1 provides a list of potential accommodations that can be implemented in the classroom.

TABLE 3.1 Sample Accommodations

Learning Environment

- Notify when a change occurs in routine, such as safety drills
- Use of noise-canceling devices
- Closed captioning
- Access to a calm or quiet space when students are overwhelmed
- Scheduled or "as needed" breaks
- Preferential seating (e.g., away from distractions, close to teacher or board)
- Access to sensory tools (e.g., fidgets, floor pedals)
- Small group or one-on-one with teacher or instructor to introduce, teach, and review concepts
- Behavior aids (e.g., cue cards, self-monitoring device)

Classroom Materials

- Use of computer or other device to complete written work
- Read aloud or audiobook
- Large print or braille
- Instruction provided in alternative or multiple modes such as visual and auditory
- Record lecture
- Teacher notes, summaries of key information
- Use of calculator
- Graphic organizers

Assignments

- Extended time to complete work
- Check-ins with teacher to ensure understanding of assignment and material
- Self-monitoring to gauge work completion
- Set expectations with a model or rubric
- Fewer questions or problems
- Scaffolding such as providing page numbers where answers can be found
- Option for teacher or teacher aide to scribe
- Option to use on-screen readers

Assessments/Test

- Extended time to complete a test (time and a half, split over more than one day)
- Give one page of the test at a time
- Reduce the number of questions or problems per page
- Read items on the test aloud
- Highlight or otherwise indicate key information on an examination
- Include a word bank with key vocabulary
- Assess in small groups
- Alternative location for the test

Adapted from McGlynn & Kelly, 2019

Postsecondary and Vocational Schools

Section 504 extends protections for students with disabilities into adulthood when the student completes secondary school. In postsecondary and vocational schools, the school, college, or university must provide eligible students with appropriate accommodations, aids, and services that allow students with disabilities to access the school's programs. However, schools are not required to provide support that will result in a significant alteration to the program's content and requirements (U.S. Department of Education OCR, 2020b).

In sum, while the definition of disabilities in Section 504 is broad and the benefits extend to all levels of education, for students with disabilities at the K–12 grade level these are minimal (accommodations) because Section 504 is an access law that prohibits discrimination; it is not a special education law, per se. Similar to the ADAA, Section 504 gives individuals access to services and places that other people without disabilities have access to as part of their daily living. While both disability laws have a broad definition and should, in theory, benefit a large segment of the population, the fact that these two federal laws have no funding attached to them minimizes the level of importance in the daily lives of students with disabilities in K–12 grades. Finally, the educational benefits that are associated with the two antidiscrimination disability laws are more about access than they are about direct educational programming.

Individuals with Disabilities Education Improvement Act

The **Individuals with Disabilities Education Improvement Act (IDEA)** is the federal law which focuses on the education of students with disabilities from early interventions (birth to age 2) through preschool to secondary school (ages 3–21). The IDEA provides guidance to states and public agencies on how to provide early interventions and special education and related services to more than 7.5 million eligible toddlers, children, and youth with disabilities. The IDEA is the most relevant federal law concerning students with disabilities, since it provides regulations, processes, and procedures for how students with disabilities are identified, evaluated, serviced, and disciplined in schools. As its name suggests, the IDEA is a special education law. It is important to note that as of 2018, approximately 95% of students with disabilities, ages 6–21, are served in general education, also referred to as "regular" or public schools (U.S. Department of Education, National Center for Education Statistics [NCES], 2021). This means that general education teachers in public schools will have students with disabilities participating in their classrooms.

> *General education teachers in public schools will have students with disabilities participating in their classrooms.*

The Purpose of the IDEA

The purpose of IDEA is to ensure that students with disabilities are provided with the accommodations, modifications and services which will best meet their individual educational needs. Where **accommodations** refer to *how* students learn, **modifications** refer to *what* students learn. Additionally, **services** refer to the specially designed instruction (SDI) that support student IEP goals, and includes information on where student receive SDI (general education or special education setting), how often the SDI takes place, and who is responsible for the SDI (special education teacher, speech language pathologist, other service providers). Congress's statement in the law is as follows:

> Disability is a natural part of the human experience and in no way diminishes the right of individuals to participate in or contribute to society. Improving educational results for children

with disabilities is an essential element of our national policy of ensuring equality of opportunity, full participation, independent living, and economic self-sufficiency for individuals with disabilities. (IDEA §(c) (1), 2004)

The IDEA applies to students in preschool, elementary, and secondary school. Of note, if a student with a disability remains in school past the age of 18, special education services will continue as long as they are in secondary school. Once the student finishes secondary school, special education services do not extend into postsecondary settings such as colleges, universities, trade schools, employment, or independent living.

Major Provision of the IDEA

The IDEA has **due process and procedural safeguards** in place to resolve any disputes that arise between parents and school at any step of the special education referral and service delivery process. Of note, the procedural safeguards can be activated by parents and by schools. Through the provision of **Child Find**, the IDEA requires schools to identify and evaluate students whose presumed or evident disabilities may have a negative effect on their academic success. Once these students are evaluated and if they are found eligible for special education services, IDEA provides them with a **free appropriate public education (FAPE)**. The **individualized education program (IEP)** is the mechanism by which FAPE is rendered. The *A* for appropriate in FAPE is detailed in the individualization of each IEP for each student. An IEP is not appropriate unless it is customized for every student. Once the IEP, a legally binding document, is written, schools are instructed to consider where the goals within the IEP will have the best chance at being met. Schools are expected to provide special education, as indicated in each student's IEP, in the **least restrictive environment (LRE)**. IDEA assumes that every student with an IEP will begin in the general education setting with general education peers to the fullest extent possible. However, the IDEA also stipulates that students with disabilities should be in the general education classroom as long as there is educational benefit. If the student is not learning in the general education setting, then an alternative placement setting must be considered. The five related provisions (Due Process and Procedural Safeguards, Child Find, FAPE, IEP, LRE) are discussed in the following sections. The process of conflict resolution will be discussed in the procedural safeguards and due process provision. However, at the end of this section, we provide an example of how conflict may arise between parent and school personnel at each step to illustrate the types of disagreements that might arise in each step of the special education process.

Due Process and Procedural Safeguards

The IDEA promotes collaboration between schools and parents in all aspects of decision-making on behalf of students with disabilities. However, under the IDEA's due process and procedural safeguards provision, the parents and guardians of children with disabilities as well as the schools have a legal mechanism to disagree with one another at any step of the special education process. For example, under the procedural safeguards provision, parents have the right to be informed

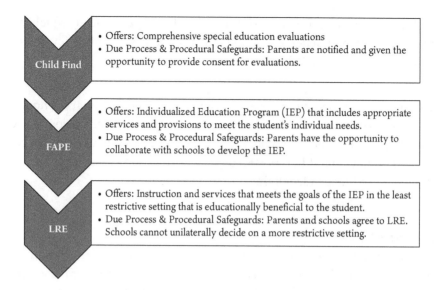

FIGURE 3.1 Special education process

when the school is considering a special education evaluation, and they have the right to request a special education evaluation at any time. Schools must provide written notice to parents and do their best to obtain written consent before the student is evaluated for special education. Additionally, under due process, parents have the right to disagree with provisions, services, and goals that are included in a student's IEP.

Child Find

As previously stated in Chapter 1, prior to the passage of a federal special education law, there were many children with disabilities who did not attend school. Knowing that children with disabilities had been previously excluded from public schooling, policy makers charged schools to find the children who were not in school. Thus, the Child Find provision seeks to find and evaluate students whose academic difficulties may be due to a disability. Figure 3.1 shows that Child Find is often the first step of the special education process. General education teachers are usually the ones to initiate a referral for evaluation for school-aged children. This makes sense, as general education teachers have the most exposure throughout the school day. However, parents also have the right to request an evaluation of their child. We discuss the evaluation and determination process in greater detail in Chapter 4. Disputes between parents and schools can arise at the Child Find level if a parent does not give written consent for special education evaluation or if the school does not comply with a parent's request to evaluate a student. In either case, procedural safeguards can be activated by either the school or the parent in the special education evaluation process.

Free Appropriate Public Education

If a student is found eligible for special education, the IDEA provides students with disabilities a **Free Appropriate Public Education (FAPE)**. The FAPE provision in the IDEA guarantees that the unique needs of each student with a disability will be addressed in a personalized manner through the IEP. That includes special education and related services which will best meet the student's needs at no cost to their families (IDEA, 2004). The commitment to educate students with disabilities is such in the IDEA that services are guaranteed to extend to settings outside of school when the student, for a variety of reasons, is not in school. For example, if a student is suspended for more than 10 days, the school is required to continue to provide the student with special education services (homebound services) or to make up those services (compensatory services). Additionally, if a student is in a hospital or in a juvenile correctional facility, they continue to be entitled to special education in those settings.

Individualized Education Program

The **Individualized Education Program (IEP)** is the mechanism by which students with disabilities receive FAPE. The IEP provides the list of provisions, such as accommodations, modifications, and services, that will best meet the individual needs of the student. **Accommodations** refers to the changes made in the learning environment and a description of how assignments and assessments are completed. **Modifications** are changes to the content or the skills required to complete educational tasks (McGlynn & Kelly, 2019). **Services** refers to assistance or aid provided by qualified individuals, such as a special education teacher, speech and language pathologist (SLP), physical therapist (PT), or occupational therapist (OT).

Additionally, the IEP provides goals related to the needs of individual students. These include academic goals, speech and language goals, and physical goals related to OT- and PT-related services (handwriting, traveling through the school), but may also include sensory, social-emotional, and behavioral goals. The goals are based on grade-level state standards and include specially designed instruction which will help students meet those goals. Progress monitoring is completed throughout the school year to determine if students are making progress toward their goals. The IEP team meets at a minimum of one time per year at the annual case conference to review goals and determine what changes need to be made to the IEP.

The IEP is developed by the IEP team, which includes the parents or guardians of the child, the child when appropriate, at least one general education teacher if the child is or may be participating in the general education setting, a representative of the public agency, such as a building or district administrator, a special educator, and any relevant service providers (IDEA, 2004). The IEP is a living document, and it can be modified or changed at any time with consent from the legal guardians.

Least Restrictive Environment (LRE)

The **Least Restrictive Environment (LRE)** provision refers to the extent in which it is appropriate for students with disabilities to participate in the general education setting with general education peers. The IDEA directs schools to always begin with the assumption that students will be educated in the general education classroom unless it is not beneficial to the student with a disability. As such, removal of students with disabilities from the general education environment should only occur when the "nature or severity" of the disability manifests in such a way that a student's needs cannot be met within the general education environment (IDEA, 2004). This decision is made by a student's team, which includes their parents or legal guardians, and is not a unilateral decision made by one entity. When students with disabilities do not benefit from instruction in the general education classroom, by law, schools must offer a range of placement alternatives for the student with disabilities. The Continuum of Alternative Placement and Services (CAPS) includes resource rooms, special education classrooms, special education day schools, homebound education, hospitals, and residential institutions, such as treatment facilities and correctional facilities. The amount of time spent with their general education peers in instruction, during electives, or less structured times (recess, cafeteria) varies based on the needs of the student. It should be noted that most students with disabilities (64%) participate in the general education 80% or more of the day (NCES, 2021).

Below, Table 3.2 uses the Ask-Read-Tell method to examine a court case involving a parent disagreement with the public school about appropriate goals.

TABLE 3.2 FAPE Case Study: *Endrew F. v. Douglas County*

ASK

- What are the provisions under FAPE?
  - A. at public expense, under public supervision and direction, and without charge;
  - B. meet standards of the state educational agency;
  - C. appropriate preschool, elementary, or secondary school education in the state involved; and
  - D. in conformity with the individualized education program. (IDEA, 20 U.S.C. §1401 [a][9][A–D])

READ

- The facts of the case:
  - Endrew F. is a student with autism and his parents were concerned that Endrew's academic and function progress had stalled.
  - Endrew received an IEP through Douglas County from preschool to 4th grade.
  - The 5th grade IEP resembled those from previous years.
  - Endrew's parents removed him from public school and enrolled him in a private school that was specialized.
  - Endrew made significant progress.
  - Endrew's parents were later presented with a new 5th-grade IEP, but his parents felt it was inadequate to meet Endrew's needs and sought reimbursement for Endrew's private school tuition.
- Parents' Position: Recent IEPs were largely the same and Endrew made no progress toward his goals and objectives.
- School's Position: Although Endrew did not make the level of progress in Douglas County that he had at the private school, he did make some progress.

TELL

- Was FAPE violated, and should the district reimburse Endrew's parents?
- Was FAPE provided by Douglas County? Explain your response.
- Should the district reimburse Endrew's parents for tuition to the private school? Explain your response.

What did the courts decide?

Colorado Department of Education (CDOE) denied the claim. The Federal District Court and Tenth Circuit upheld the decision of the CDOE. However, the US Supreme Court heard the case and, in a unanimous decision, sent the case back to the Tenth Circuit to be retried (Yell & Bateman, 2017). A federal judge determined that the district should reimburse Endrew's parents, and they were awarded $1.32 million (ASHA Letter, 2018).

School Discipline

As discussed in Chapter 2, the IDEA includes provisions related to discipling students with disabilities; the process is called Manifestation Determination (MD) in the IDEA. The MD is the process schools must follow to determine if the student's misbehavior is related to his or her disability. In the process of disciplining a student with a disability, a manifestation determination meeting is held with the student's IEP team to determine if the change of placement is appropriate. The main purpose of a manifestation determination meeting it to determine whether the student is receiving the appropriate services (FAPE) in the least restrictive environment (LRE) that best meets the needs of the student. When students with disabilities are disciplined by being removed from school, the IDEA mandates that special education services must continue if students are removed from school for more than 10 days, resulting in a change of placement. Change of placement not only refers to an alternative education setting, such as a homebound placement or alternative school setting, but also refers to the 10 or more cumulative days' removal from school. If the pattern of behavior that results in removal from school is related to the student's disability or is related to the provisions of the IEP not being implemented as written, then it is determined that the behavior is related to, or is a manifestation of, the student's disability, and a change of placement is not recommended. Whether or not the pattern of behavior and school removal are directly related to the student's disability, the IEP team is required to develop a behavior intervention plan with the purpose of allowing the student to participate in the general education environment to the fullest extent possible. The behavior intervention plan should be based on the student's social-emotional and behavioral needs.

> *Whether or not the pattern of behavior and school removal are directly related to the student's disability, the IEP team is required to develop a behavior intervention plan.*

Transition Goals

The provisions of IDEA only extend through secondary schools. However, as discussed in Chapter 2, schools are responsible for helping students with disabilities transition from secondary school to postsecondary school or employment. This is accomplished through transition goals and services. Section 300.43 of the IDEA (2004) defines transition services as a coordinated set of activities that are designed to be a part of a results-oriented, or goal-oriented, process that is focused on academic and functional achievements that will help the student move from school-related activities to post-school-related activities, such as behaviors related to finding and maintaining employment, continuing education, independent living, and participating in the community.

Transition services are based on the needs, strengths, preferences, and interests of the student. These services include specially designed instruction, related services, such as occupational therapy or physical therapy, community experiences, and independent living tasks. Community experiences can include learning about their rights under the ADAA or Section 504, registering to vote, participating in community events like church or volunteer opportunities, or getting a library card.

Independent living tasks may include such activities as grocery shopping, doing laundry, making a budget, or cooking.

Summary

In this chapter, we have discussed the three main federal disability laws and have noted that the IDEA is the only federal special education law. Section 504 and ADAAA are antidiscrimination (or access) laws that prohibit discrimination against individuals with disabilities. Of all the laws discussed in this chapter, the ADAAA is the broadest federal civil rights law that addresses individuals with disabilities and addresses all individuals with disabilities, whether or not they qualify under the IDEA and whether or not federal funding is involved like in Section 504. While Section 504 and the ADAAA have broader definitions of disabilities, the IDEA provides more services and benefits for students with disabilities in K–12 grades. In addition, it is important to note that each state also has its own version of special education law, and each district has its own procedures for carrying out the special education service delivery process. However, state and district level regulations must meet the minimum requirements of the federal special education law (i.e., the IDEA).

Test Your Knowledge

1. Which of the three disability laws is most relevant for special education?
2. Define accommodations, modifications, and services.
   a. Which are included in a 504 plan?
   b. Which are included in an IEP?
3. What are general education teachers responsible for providing in accommodations, modifications, and services for students with IEPs or 504 plans?
4. Can the school unilaterally decide a student with a disability be moved to a more restrictive environment (homebound, alternative school, etc.) because of student misbehavior? Why, or why not?
5. Create a visual (e.g., table or Venn diagram) that shows the similarities and differences between the IDEA, Section 504, and the ADAAA. How are these laws similar? How do they differ?

Apply Your Knowledge

In March of 2020, schools were closed nationwide in response to the COVID-19 global pandemic. Most IEPs and 504 plans were written in compliance with instructions, accommodations, modifications, and services being provided in person.

Ask

Ask yourself the following questions to help guide your reading.

- Since it was unclear when students would return to in-person learning, were schools required to rewrite IEPs and 504 plans to align with virtual or distance learning?
- In general, did virtual or distance learning violate FAPE?
- In general, did virtual or distance learning violate LRE?

Read

Re-read the following sections.

- Individuals with Disabilities Act: Individualized Education Programs, Free Appropriate Public Education, and Least Restrictive Environment (p. 28)
- Section 504 of the Rehabilitation Act: Section 504 Purpose, Section 504 in Public Schools, and Section 504 Plans (p. 25)

Tell

Tell your response.

- Based on the questions posed in ASK and the sections provided in READ, answer the following question: *How were students with disabilities' federal and civil rights (FAPE and LRE) impacted by school closures?*

References

Americans with Disabilities Act [ADA] of 1990, Pub. L. No. 101-336, §12101, 104 Stat. 328 (2008). Retrieved July 12, 2021, from https://www.ada.gov/pubs/adastatute08.htm#12101b

ASHA Letter. (2018). "Endrew" case settles for $1.3 million. *News in Brief*, September 2018. Retrieved July 12, 2021, from https://doi.org/10.1044/leader.NIB2.23092018.10

Endrew F., a Minor, by and Through His Parents and Next Friends, Joseph F. et al. v. Douglas County School District RE–1, 64 IDELR 38, (D., Co. 2014), 580 U.S. _____ (2017).

Hulett, K. E. (2009) *Legal aspects of special education*. Pearson.

Individuals With Disabilities Education Act, 20 U.S.C. §§300, 1400, 1412. (2004).

McGlynn, K., & Kelly, J. (2019) Adaptations, modifications, and accommodations. *National Science Teachers Association, 43*(30), 36–41. https://www.jstor.org/stable/10.2307/26899082

National Center for Education Statistics (NCES). (2021). *Digest of education statistics, 2019* (NCES 2021-009), Chapter 2. https://nces.ed.gov/pubs2021/2021009.pdf

U.S. Department of Education (U.S. DOE). (1999) IDEA '97 provisions of special interest to administrators. Topic brief. Retrieved July 12, 2021, from https://www2.ed.gov/policy/speced/leg/idea/brief14.html

U.S. Department of Education (U.S. DOE). (2007). No child left behind behavior: Help for students and their families. https://www2.ed.gov/parents/academic/involve/2006toolkit/nclb-en.html

U.S. Department of Education (U.S. DOE). (2015) Every student succeeds act (ESSA). https://www.ed.gov/essa?src=ft

U.S. Department of Education (U.S. DOE). (2017). June 30, 2017 (82 FR 29755). https://sites.ed.gov/idea/idea-files/june-30-2017-82-fr-29755/

U.S. Department of Education Office of Civil Rights. (2020a). Americans with disabilities act. https://www2.ed.gov/about/offices/list/ocr/docs/hq9805.html

U.S. Department of Education Office of Civil Rights. (2020b). Protecting students with disabilities. https://www2.ed.gov/about/offices/list/ocr/504faq.html

U.S. Department of Health and Human Services Department of Civil Rights. (1978). Section 504 of the Rehabilitation Act of 1973. https://www.hhs.gov/sites/default/files/ocr/civilrights/resources/fact-sheets/504.pdf

U.S. Department of Labor. (n.d.). Section 504, Rehabilitation Act of 1973. https://www.dol.gov/agencies/oasam/centers-offices/civil-rights-center/statutes/section-504-rehabilitation-act-of-1973

Yell, M., & Bateman, D. (2017). Endrew F. v. Douglas County school district (2017): FAPE and the U.S. Supreme Court. *Teaching Exceptional Children*. doi: 10.1177/0040059917721116

Zirkel, P., Granthom, M., & Lovato, L. (2012). Section 504 and student health problems: The pivotal position of the school nurse. *The Journal of School Nursing, 28*(6), 423–432. doi:10.1177/1059840512449358

Federal Process for Evaluation and Eligibility for Special Education Services

Chapter 4 discusses the special education referral process as discussed in the Individuals with Disabilities Education Improvement Act (IDEA, 2004) as well as the roles and responsibilities of general education and special education teachers in the process. As discussed in Chapter 3, the Child Find provision of the IDEA (2004) seeks to find and evaluate students whose academic difficulties may be due to a disability. General education teachers are usually the ones to initiate a referral for evaluation for school-aged children. This makes sense, as general education teachers have the most exposure to students throughout the school day and can see more readily when students struggle academically. However, the IDEA also grants parents or guardians the right to request an evaluation for their child if parents or guardians are concerned that their child might have a disability. It is important to note that the majority of initial referrals and initial evaluations occur at the elementary school level. However, initial evaluations do occur at the secondary level. Nonetheless, general education teachers at all levels are often involved in the cases of reevaluations, making it important for general educators to know the process of evaluation and eligibility criteria that students must meet to receive special education services.

In this chapter, readers will:

- Read the definitions and criteria for the 13 categories of special education in the IDEA (2004 §300.8);

All Future Educators
The evaluation process is a highly collaborative process between educators, parents or guardians, and other trained professionals.

Elementary General Education
Elementary schoolteachers are often the source of initial evaluation referrals and provide in-depth information about student academic functioning and growth.

Secondary General Education
Although initial evaluations are less common at the secondary level, secondary school teachers are required to refer students for evaluation if they suspect a disability may be impacting student functioning.

Special Education
Special educators provide unique insight into how the characteristics associated with each disability may impact student learning and, through the collaborative process, will develop appropriate strategies and instruction to help students meet their educational goals.

Undergraduates Interested in Disability Laws
Parents and guardians have the right to refuse evaluations and services; however, there are procedural safeguards schools can follow to contest parental refusal. In such cases, hearing officers who are trained in special education law may be called upon to determine what is in the best interest of the child.

- Learn the federal special education referral and evaluation process;
- Identify and define key terms: **related services**, **IEP team**, **high-incidence disability**, **low-incidence disability**, **initial evaluation**, **reevaluation**, and **triennial review**.

After reading this chapter, readers will:

- Understand their roles and responsibilities in the special education evaluation process;
- Develop an understanding of the legal rights of parents and students in the special education referral and evaluation process;
- Discuss the importance of parents and guardians in the special education referral and evaluation process.

The Process of Referral to Special Education

A referral for an educational evaluation is the first step in the special education referral process. Once referred for evaluation, the student is evaluated by a team of school professionals to determine if the student is eligible to receive special education and related services. **Special education** is specially designed instruction that meets the unique characteristics and needs of students with disabilities. **Related services** refer to special education services that support the developmental, corrective, or transportation needs of students with disabilities so that they may benefit from special education. This includes speech and language services, assistive technology, mental health services, medical services, services that support fine and gross motor skills, or sensory concerns (IDEA, 2004, §300.34). First, we list and describe the 13 disability categories listed as recognized in the IDEA (2004, 300.8). Knowing the basic characteristics and criteria of each special education disability can help guide referrals for educational evaluations. Second, we discuss the roles and responsibilities of the Individual Education Program (IEP) team. The different members of the IEP team each bring a unique perspective to the collaborative process. Lastly, we provide an overview of the referral and evaluation process, highlighting the role and responsibilities of special education and general education teachers.

Special Education Disability Categories

The IDEA recognizes 13 categories of disability (§300.8). It is important to know them and their characteristics prior to referring a student for special education evaluation. The 13 categories of disabilities listed in the IDEA are as follows in order by incident rate (NCES, 2022); (1) specific learning disability; (2) speech or language impairment; (3) other health impairment; (4) autism; (5) developmental delay; (6) intellectual disability; (7) emotional disturbance; (8) multiple disabilities; (9) hearing impairment; (10) orthopedic impairment; (11) visual impairments; (12) traumatic brain injury; and (13) deaf-blindness.

According to the NCES (2022), over 95% of all students with disabilities were found to be eligible for the following disability categories: specific learning disability, speech or language impairment, other health impairment, autism, developmental delay, intellectual disability, and emotional disability.

These are considered **high-incidence** areas of disabilities and represent those students who will most likely receive accommodations and modifications in general education settings.

According to the NCES (2022), less than 5% of all students with disabilities were found eligible for the following areas of disabilities: multiple disabilities, hearing impairments, and orthopedic impairments. Less than 1% of students with disabilities in total were found eligible as students with visual impairments, deaf-blindness, or traumatic brain injury. These are considered **low-incidence** areas of disabilities and represent those with the most profound needs who are likely being provided with special education services from multiple service providers. While it is the goal to fully include students with disabilities in general education classrooms along with their non-disabled peers, when possible, students with more severe educational needs are provided with services by professionals with areas of expertise outside of the general education curriculum. These professionals have training focused on students with more intensive needs.

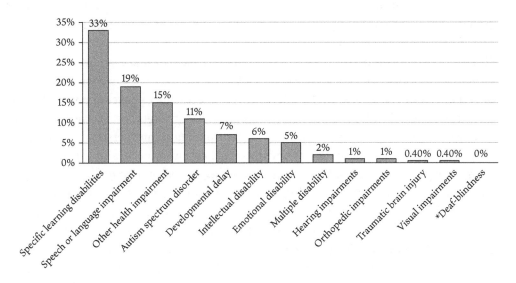

FIGURE 4.1 Percentage of students with disabilities by category, per NCES 2022

Below is a description of the definition and criteria for each of the 13 categories of disabilities outlined in the IDEA (2004, §300.8):

- **Specific learning disabilities (SLD)** refers to an impairment in one or more psychological or cognitive functions responsible for understanding language, written or spoken, which impact education performance in the areas of reading, writing, mathematics, oral expression or listening comprehension, and are not primarily due to another area of disability. However, specific learning disabilities may co-occur or be comorbid with other disabilities.
- **Speech or language impairments (SLI)** deals with impairments in receptive (understanding) language or expressive (written and spoken) language, or impairments in producing speech sounds.
- **Other health impairment (OHI)** refers to conditions that impact alertness, strength, and vitality in the learning environment and which impact learning to a marked degree. This is most commonly used in schools for students with attention deficit hyperactivity disorder (ADHD) who are eligible for special education and related services. However, any chronic

medical condition that impacts the ability to sustain attention on relevant stimuli is included in this category. This includes, but is not limited to, such medical conditions like asthma, sickle cell anemia, cancer, diabetes, or epilepsy.

- **Autism spectrum disorder (ASD)** is a lifelong developmental disability that is associated with the following characteristics: (1) social interaction and communication problems; (2) restricted and repetitive patterns of behaviors, interests, or activities; and (3) unusual responses to sensory experiences.
- **Developmental delay** applies only to students ages 3–9. Students with developmental delays demonstrate a significant delay in at least one or demonstrate moderate delays in at least two of the following areas: (1) gross or fine motor development; (2) cognitive development; (3) receptive or expressive language development; (4) social and emotional development; and (5) adaptive skills, such as self-help.
- **Intellectual disabilities** refer to significant delays in cognitive or intellectual functioning (intelligence quotients [IQ] of 70 or less) and in adaptive skills. Intellectual disabilities manifest in early childhood.
- **Emotional disturbance** deals with the inability to learn or make progress that cannot be explained by cognitive ability, sensory, or other health factors. Emotional disabilities are associated with at least one of the following: (1) a tendency to develop physical symptoms or fears associated with personal or school problems; (2) general pervasive mood of unhappiness or depression; (3) an inability to build or maintain interpersonal relationships; (4) inappropriate feelings or behaviors under normal circumstances; and (5) episodes of psychosis. Characteristics must be present over a long period of time to a marked degree and must impact educational functioning. It is important to note here that the federal law uses the term "emotional disturbance"; however, due to the negative connotation of the word *disturbance*, most states and experts in the field use the term *emotional disability*.
- **Multiple disabilities** refers to co-occurring conditions in one student which cause severe education needs, one of which must include an intellectual disability, that their needs cannot be explained by solely one area of disability. This does not include students with deaf-blindness.
- **Hearing impairment and deafness** refers to an impairment of hearing that can be permanent or that fluctuates; it adversely impacts learning and educational performance, but not to such a marked degree to be considered deafness. Deafness refers to a condition that is so profound that processing information through hearing, both with and without amplification, adversely impacts learning and educational performance.
- **Orthopedic impairment** concerns an impairment in the bones or muscles that adversely impact learning and education performance.
- **Traumatic brain injury** refers to an injury that is acquired to the brain from an external force (open or closed injury), which results in an impairment in one or more area, including cognitive functioning, physical functioning, communication, or social emotional functioning.
- **Visual impairment** relates to an impairment in vision that, even with correction, adversely impacts learning and educational performance.
- **Deaf-blindness** refers to a co-occurring visual and hearing impairment condition that adversely impacts communication, developmental, and educational needs which cannot be explained solely by deafness or blindness.

IEP Team

The IDEA requires collaboration in all educational planning of students with disabilities. The Individualized Education Program (IEP) team, sometimes also called the multidisciplinary team or Child Study Team, is responsible for making educational decisions for students with disabilities. This includes determining when a student is eligible for special education, under what category or categories the student is eligible for services, as well as the modifications, accommodations, goals, specially designed instruction, and other related services that go into the IEP. The minimum required members of an IEP team are outlined in the IDEA (2004, §1414) and includes parents or legal guardians and the student as it is possible and appropriate. The student only is included in the IEP meeting at the secondary level to provide students with the opportunity to have input in their own educational experience and to discuss transition goals. The special education teacher, a representative of the local education agency (LEA), and any related service providers are also members of the team. Additionally, at least one regular or general education teacher is required when the student participates in the regular or general education environment. The LEA is knowledgeable about the general education curriculum and resources and is typically a building level or district level administrator such as a school principal. Related service providers refer to occupational therapists, physical therapists, speech and language pathologists, and any other certified staff member providing services to the student with disabilities. For IEP meetings that include reviewing the results of special education evaluations, individuals who are licensed to interpret the instructional implications of evaluation results, such as occupational therapists, physical therapists, speech and language pathologists, and school psychologists, must be included. When students receive services from outside agencies like mental health professionals or a state-assigned caseworker, they may also be part of the IEP team.

Types of Referrals

There are two types of referrals for special education evaluations. The first is the **initial evaluation**. An initial evaluation referral is a request to evaluate students who are not yet receiving special education services for special education eligibility and services. This applies to students who have never been evaluated, were previously evaluated but did not qualify for special education, and for students who did receive services in the past but were later found to no longer be eligible for special education. The second type of referral is **reevaluation**. Reevaluation referrals are requests to evaluate students who are currently receiving special education services to determine if the student continues to qualify for special education, to determine if the student qualifies under a different or additional category of special education, and to determine if the student requires assistive technology or related services. In addition to evaluation referrals, a **triennial review** (a review every three years) is required to be conducted to inform the IEP team of current needs of students and to determine if a reevaluation referral is necessary to provide more information. Both the parent or guardian and the local education agency must agree that a reevaluation is not warranted (IDEA, 2004, §1414).

Process for Special Education Evaluations

This section of the chapter describes the process for determining whether students are eligible for special education. This is a four-step process: (1) referring students for an evaluation; (2) signed informed consent; (3) comprehensive evaluation; and (4) eligibility determination. In this section, we will also discuss the federal timelines for the special education evaluation process. However, state-mandated timelines may differ. It is the responsibility of the professional to adhere to the special education laws in their state.

Referring Students for Evaluation

Parents or guardians and a representative from a state agency or local educational agency may initiate a request for an initial evaluation or reevaluation (IDEA, 2004, §1414). The IDEA does not give specific guidance on how long state and local agencies must respond to referrals for evaluation, only that it needs to be within a "reasonable" time frame.

Regardless of who initiates the referral for special education evaluation and whether it is an initial evaluation or reevaluation, the role and responsibility of the general education teacher is to provide information on student educational, social-emotional, and behavioral functioning in the general education setting. General education teachers, especially at the elementary school level, are often the source of initial evaluation referrals, as discussed in previous chapters. Special education and general education teachers at all grade levels can provide information about student relationships with peers and other adults, patterns in mood and behavior, student motivation, and ability to begin tasks independently.

> *The role and responsibility of the general education teacher is to provide information on student educational, social-emotional, and behavioral functioning in the general education setting.*

For initial evaluations, the role and responsibilities of special education teachers may vary from state to state, district to district, or even grade level to grade level. At the elementary school level, special education teachers are often involved in schoolwide behavioral interventions (see Chapter 7) and would likely be able to provide in-depth information about student academic functioning and growth compared to their same-grade non-disabled peers. Special education teachers are often the ones making referrals for reevaluation.

Signed Informed Consent

An informed consent includes a description of the processes and procedures included in the evaluation (IDEA, 2004, §300.300). The IDEA (§300.300) stipulates that a school must make reasonable efforts to obtain a signed informed consent from a parent or guardian before an evaluation is conducted. The IDEA, however, does not provide guidance on what is considered reasonable. In cases where the parent or guardian does not respond to a school's reasonable efforts to obtain signed informed consent, an evaluation can take place without it. In some cases where a parent objects to the student being evaluated, school personnel can seek to conduct the evaluation by appealing to a hearing officer. If the hearing officer sides with a school's request to conduct an evaluation, the school can move forward with the evaluation without parental consent. Nonetheless, it is important to state here that consent to evaluate a student does not mean that a parent has to accept special education or related services or alternative placement if the student qualifies for special education services. Signed informed consent for evaluation is merely a consent for an evaluation to be completed. If a general education or special education teacher receives a signed informed consent from a parent or guardian, it is their responsibility to submit the consent to the person responsible for processing the consent.

Comprehensive Evaluations

Once signed informed consent is obtained, the evaluation timeline begins. According to the IDEA (2004), schools have 60 days to complete the comprehensive evaluation. In the IDEA, *60 days* refers to calendar days, including weekends and holidays, unless otherwise specified (IDEA, §1414). A comprehensive evaluation includes assessment tools and strategies, or measures, which are designed to gather relevant functional, developmental, and academic information, which includes input from the parent (IDEA; §1414). No single measure can be used to determine whether a student is eligible for special education or to determine special education and related services. Additionally, measures should be nondiscriminatory and not racially or culturally biased.

Special education and general education teachers' responsibilities during the evaluation process include communicating with relevant IEP team members about student availability for completing evaluation measures and observations. Additionally, general education teachers may be asked to complete questionnaires or rating scales, provide student work samples, and complete interviews with IEP team members about the student going through the evaluation process. Special education teachers may be required to complete observations and conduct interviews as part of the evaluation process.

Determination of Eligibility Conference

Once the comprehensive evaluation is completed, the IEP team gathers to review the results of the evaluation and discuss whether the student meets criteria for special education under one or more of the disability categories described in the IDEA. Note the language that is used in this chapter. In special education terms, students are identified with disabilities. This is not to be confused with a diagnosis, which is a medical term. The meeting must be held no later than the 60th day of the school receiving signed consent. According to the IDEA (2004, §1414), parents are provided with notice of meeting at least five days prior to the meeting and are provided with the evaluation report, if requested, no more than three days before the meeting. In cases where parents or guardians did not provide signed informed consent for an evaluation, but the school was able to move forward with the evaluation, parents or guardians still retain to the right to decline or to accept special education services at this point.

If the IEP team determines a student is eligible for special education, the IEP team develops an individualized education program (IEP), specific to the student's individual needs, which constitutes the free appropriate public education (FAPE) principle of the IDEA. FAPE includes special education and related services, accommodations, modifications (See Chapter 3, IEPs), educational goals, and the specially designed instruction to help students meet their IEP goals. The definition of special education is the specially designed instruction provided in the IEP and refers to the "who, what, when, and where" of instruction (see Table 4.1) that will be provided to meet the unique needs of the student at no cost to the parent.

TABLE 4.1 The "Who, What, When, Where" of Specially Designed Instruction

Who is providing the service?	
Refers to appropriate service providers responsible for providing and documenting the service.	Examples: Special education teacher, related service provided such as speech and language pathologist, general education teacher, or school counselor.
What is the service that is being provided?	
Refers to appropriate services that will address the skill.	Examples: Phonics (reading related), speech services, small-group instruction, or school-based mental health or behavioral services.
When is the service being provided?	
Refers to the amount of time the student will receive the service: daily, weekly, or within a specified time period.	Examples: 3 days per week, 20 minutes per day, 60 minutes a week, or 9 hours during a 9-week semester.
Where are the services being provided?	
Refers to the environment in which the services are being provided and informs LRE in terms of time spent in general education classrooms or with general education peers.	Examples for general education: In the general education classroom or paired with general education peers with similar needs in small groups. Examples for special education: In special education classroom or other setting, away from general education peers. Services can be provided individually, in small groups, or whole class with special education peers.

If the IEP team determines that a student does not meet criteria for special education under any of the disability categories of the IDEA, the team may consider if the student meets criteria for a disability as discussed in Section 504 of the Rehabilitation Act. The IEP team then can recommend that a 504 plan be created and implemented. It must be restated here that a 504 plan is not the same as the IEP. Only the IEP provides special education to students with disabilities.

IEP educational goals are based on the student's current level of functioning and provide a goal that is **s**pecific, **m**easurable, **a**chievable, **r**esourced, and **t**imebound (SMART). A specific goal refers to a goal that provides a specific skill rather than a general one. A measurable goal includes a goal which can be observed, counted, or otherwise assessed. IEP educational goals are also within reach of the student's abilities based on current level of functioning (achievable) and includes the specially designed instruction (resourced). Additionally, IEP goals are time oriented, or timebound, meaning there is a set amount time in which the goals may realistically be achieved. At the end of the set time, if the goal is not achieved, the team can adjust the goal or adjust the supports to better meet the needs of the student. We will discuss goal setting in more detail in chapters related to classroom interventions and strategies.

Once the IEP is written, the IEP team will also discuss placement options. In public school settings, this typically takes the form of support in general education, special education classrooms and programs, or the hybrid model, which includes both time spent in general education as well as in special education. Inclusion support in general education means students are receiving any relevant services or supports, such as accommodation and modifications in the general education setting for 80% or more of their day. This means that in the cases in which the IEP team places a student with disabilities in the general education classroom to receive their special education in the education setting, general education teachers are responsible for the educational programming of students with disabilities who have an IEP. Placing students with disabilities in the general education classroom requires coordination and collaboration with the special education teacher. To be clear, determining the least restrictive environment (LRE) for each student with a disability requires careful planning and monitoring to ensure that any placement options in the continuum of alternative placements and services (CAPS) have the best chances of meeting the goals of the student's IEP.

TABLE 4.2 Percentage of Students (Ages 3–21) with High-Incident Disabilities in General Education

Type of Disability	80%+ in General Education	40–79% in General Education	39% or Less in General Education
All	64%	18%	13%
Specific Learning Disability	72%	21%	5%
Speech or Language Impairment	88%	5%	4%
Other Health Impairment	67%	20%	9%
Autism Spectrum Disorder	40%	19%	36%
Developmental Delay	66%	19%	14%
Intellectual Disability	17%	27%	49%
Emotional Disability	50%	17%	17%

Note: Percentages rounded to the nearest whole number. Source: National Center for Education Statistics (2022). Students With Disabilities. Condition of Education. U.S. Department of Education, Institute of Education Sciences. From https://nces.ed.gov/programs/coe/indicator/cgg

Students placed in the general education classroom are the responsibility of general education teachers. As such, the general education teacher will provide information about student performance and current level of functioning. The general education teacher can provide insight on the unique dynamics of their classroom, such as peer mentors and models, instructional models and supports, and availability of resources (e.g., instructional aides, student teachers, computer programs, tutoring, etc.). It is recommended that all general educators take a strength-based approach as they teach students with disabilities. This may mean discussing how the student's strengths can support their areas of needs rather than focusing on student "weaknesses." Special education teachers will also provide information about student performance and current level of functioning, as appropriate. For reevaluations, triennial reviews and all other types of IEP meetings, special education teachers will provide progress monitoring data that is specific to student IEP goals. Additionally, special education teachers are often the primary service providers and case managers. The special education teachers are responsible for ensuring general education teachers have a copy of the student IEPs and that students are receiving their accommodations and modifications as written in the IEP across settings.

> *It is recommended that all general educators take a strength-based approach as they teach students with disabilities rather than focusing on student "weaknesses."*

Summary

Students can be identified with a disability at any stage of their learning; however, most students are identified with a disability prior to entering secondary school. Teachers or parents are most commonly those who initiate the evaluation process. Parents generally make referrals directly to the teacher, and it is the responsibility of the teacher to inform their administrators or other designated staff member to begin the referral process. Although licensed professionals are responsible for many of the features of a comprehension evaluation, teachers and parents are both vital members of the team. Teachers can speak to classroom performance and what has been done in the classroom to help support student needs. Parents and guardians can provide insight into what the student is like outside of school, as well as overall student health, developmental milestones, and exposure to academic concepts (e.g., knowing their letters and numbers) prior to entering school.

Test Your Knowledge

1. Who are the people and professionals who make up the IEP team?
2. Which disabilities are considered high incidence versus low incidence?
3. What are the differences between the two evaluations?
   a. initial evaluation referral
   b. reevaluation referral
4. Define triennial review.
5. What are the steps in the special education process?
6. Discuss the circumstances in which a school can conduct a special education evaluation without signed consent from a parent or guardian.
7. What is the role of general education and special education teachers in each step of the educational evaluation process?

Apply Your Knowledge

A student has been referred for an educational evaluation by the school to determine if they are eligible for special education and related services. The student's parent agreed over the phone to the evaluation but has not returned a signed consent.

Ask

Ask yourself the following question to help guide your reading.

- If students are found eligible for special education, are general education teachers responsible for following students' IEPs?

Read

Read the following sections.

- Evaluation Review and Determination Case Conference (p. 43) including:
  - Table 4.1 The "Who, What, When, Where" of Specially Designed Instruction (p. 44)
  - Table 4.2 Percentage of Students (Ages 3–21) with High-Incidence Disabilities in General Education (p. 45)

Tell

Tell your response.

- Based on your readings so far, are general education teachers responsible for providing at least some services to students with disabilities in their classrooms? For this question, provide the specific information from the text.

References

Individuals with Disabilities Education Act, 20 U.S.C. §§1414 (2004). Evaluations, eligibility determinations, individualized education programs, and educational placements. Retrieved from https://sites.ed.gov/idea/statute-chapter-33/subchapter-ii/1414

Individuals with Disabilities Education Act, 20 U.S.C. §300.300 (2004). Parental Consent. Retrieved from https://sites.ed.gov/idea/regs/b/d/300.300

Individuals with Disabilities Education Act, 20 U.S.C. §300.8 (2004). Child with a Disability. Retrieved from https://sites.ed.gov/idea/regs/b/a/300.8

Individuals with Disabilities Education Act, 20 U.S.C. §300 (2017). Evaluation procedures. Retrieved from https://sites.ed.gov/idea/regs/b/d/300.304

Individuals with Disabilities Education Act, 20 U.S.C. §300.34 (2017). Related Services. Retrieved from https://sites.ed.gov/idea/regs/b/a/300.34#:~:text=Related%20services%20means%20transportation%20and,services%2C%20psychological%20services%2C%20physical%20and

National Center for Education Statistics. (2022). Students with Disabilities. *Condition of Education*. U.S. Department of Education, Institute of Education Sciences. Retrieved June 10, 2022, from https://nces.ed.gov/programs/coe/indicator/cgg

Figure Credit

Fig. 4.1: Source: https://nces.ed.gov/programs/coe/indicator/cgg.

5

Educators and Parents as Partners

This chapter stresses the importance of collaboration between parents or guardians and teachers. We encourage general and special educators to shift away from the common approach of working in isolation toward collaboration when delivering special education supports to students with disabilities. As Chapter 2 indicates, when the Public Law-94 142, now called the Individuals with Disabilities Education Improvement Act (IDEA), became the special education law of the United States of America (US), schools were required to provide an individualized education program (IEP) and access to meaningful instructional experiences for each student with a disability. Prior to federal special legislation, unilateral decisions by school personnel were commonplace, which rendered students with disabilities and their parents or guardians at the mercy and goodwill of school administrators. Prior to 1975, while some states did provide some education to students with disabilities, many schools did not and could turn away students they determined unfit to benefit from their educational offerings. From the start, the IDEA has encouraged collaboration among all educators who interact with students with disabilities and has also promoted parental involvement and collaboration. In fact, the IDEA (2004) mandates a multidisciplinary (teachers, school psychologist, parents or guardians, e.g.) team approach and strictly prohibits any one person from making a unilateral decision about a student with a disability.

All Future Educators
All persons on the IEP team bring in their own expertise: general educators know the curriculum, special educators know the characteristics of students with disabilities and strategies to work with them, and parents or guardians provide a perspective of the child across time and outside of the school environment.

Elementary General Education
Identifying a student for special education services early in the academic career can help facilitate better long-term educational outcomes.

Secondary General Education
Secondary general education teachers are typically specialized in teaching one content area, whereas special education teachers must support students across content areas.

Special Education
For students with IEPs, special education teachers are usually the point of contact for other members of the IEP team and provide progress monitoring information to parents and guardians.

Undergraduates Interested in Disability Laws
Parent involvement has been a central goal in special education legislation and schools are responsible for facilitating parental involvement.

Thus, Chapter 5 urges educators to engage parents or guardians as integral members of the IEP team on behalf of students with disabilities.

In this chapter, readers will:

- Understand the distinct roles general educators and special educators play in the education of students with disabilities;
- Learn about the IDEA's requirements for parent participation and involvement;
- Learn the definition of participation, involvement, engagement, and collaboration;
- Learn about ways to increase collaboration and reduce friction between parents or guardians and school personnel;
- Learn about tips for developing and maintaining positive relationships with parents or guardians and families of students with disabilities at the elementary and high school levels.

After reading this chapter, readers will be able to discuss the:

- Benefits of collaboration between general and special educators in the education of students with disabilities;
- Unique ways in which parents or guardians of students with disabilities can contribute to the educational goals set by school personnel for students with disabilities;
- Ways school personnel can work together to treat parents or guardians not as adversaries or passive recipients of services, but as equal partners with different strengths in the education of students with disabilities.

Collaborative Decision-Making Process for Students with Disabilities

Collaboration between educators and parents or guardians of students with disabilities is not a new concept (Holdheide & Reschly, 2008). Collaboration is enshrined in the IDEA since its inception through the multidisciplinary team mandate (Ochoa, 2018). Arbitrary and unilateral decisions that impact students with disabilities are prohibited under the IDEA (Ochoa, 2018). The IDEA explicitly mandates that schools involve different school-level professionals in the decision-making process of students with disabilities. According to the IDEA, a multidisciplinary team, commonly referred to as the individualized education program (IEP) team, or the Child Study Team (Lauer, 2014), must include general educators, special educators, a bilingual educator if the student's family uses a language other than English as their primary form of communication, related service providers when appropriate, school psychologists, as needed, school administrators, a representative from the local education agency (LEA), parents or guardians, and to the extent possible, the students. Nonetheless, collaboration among educators and guardians has been a challenge (Strassfeld, 2019). Cross-professional collaboration is necessary to construct academically responsive classrooms that promote learning among students with disabilities (Hansen et al., 2020). In the next sections, we discuss the role of general education and special education teachers.

Role of General Education Teachers

General education teachers are crucial to the education and success of students with disabilities. Because the main role of the general education teacher is to develop and implement academic curricula for all students in their class (Hansen et al., 2020), the Child Find provision and the Least Restrictive Environment (LRE) provision of the IDEA both relate to the role of general educators in the education of students with disabilities. As discussed in previous chapters, the IDEA presumes that the LRE for students with disabilities is the general education classroom, unless there is a legitimate educational reason to place the student in a different setting (Holdheide & Reschly, 2008). Although both the Child Find and LRE provisions have been discussed in previous chapters, in this chapter, an emphasis is placed on the role general education teachers have in relationship to these provisions as discussed below.

The Child Find provision of the IDEA is most often met by general education teachers since approximately 80% of referrals for special education evaluation are made by general education teachers (Christopulos & Kean, 2020). Most students with disabilities, except the ones with significant and visible disabilities from childhood, begin their schooling in the general education classroom. It is the general education teacher who is most likely to be the first to notice when any student struggles to learn in the general education classroom. As such, general education teachers are the ones most likely to initiate the Child Find provision of the IDEA as discussed in Chapters 3 and 4, since they are generally the ones with the task of determining when students who do not respond to their instructional efforts need to be referred for special education evaluation. Christopulos and Kean (2020) reported that nearly 80% of all referrals made for special education evaluation were from general education teachers, and only 10% came from specialists, 5% came from parents or guardians, and 5% came from administrators. Nonetheless, many general education teachers are unaware of their role in the initiation of special education process (Ochoa, 2018). Without a referral to be evaluated, many students with disabilities remain in the general education classroom without the benefits of specialized education that IDEA guarantees for students with disabilities (Ochoa, 2018). Christopulos and Kean (2020) asserted that students with disabilities who are not identified for special education are at a cumulative risk for academic and social difficulties during their formative school years. These authors argue that students who have disabilities but are not identified suffer because they do not receive the special education assistance and protections they need. Therefore, the role of general educators in identifying students who need assistance is critical for the academic success of students with disabilities. The Child Find provision relies on general education teachers, as employees of the school, to pay attention and refer students who are struggling in their general education classrooms. Referring a student who is struggling in the general education classroom is appropriate. It is the IDEA's expectation in the Child Find provision. In fact, finding students whose disabilities prevent them from learning through the instruction provided by general education teachers is the only way that the benefits of special education can be provided to students whose academic struggles are due to disabilities (Ochoa, 2008).

> *Students with disabilities who are not identified for special education are at a cumulative risk for academic and social difficulties during their formative school years.*

Moving students with disabilities from general education classrooms and instruction is only appropriate when the severity of the student's disability and the nature of their academic needs cannot be met in the general education classroom (IDEA, 2004). According to Holdheide & Reschly (2008), the IDEA has created the expectation that public and private schools and other care facilities for children should make every effort to ensure that students with disabilities are educated with their non-disabled peers. However, if a student with a disability is not making sufficient progress or the appropriate and expected academic progress, there is nothing in the IDEA that says that students cannot be placed in other settings to learn. According to the IDEA, removal from the general education classroom to a special education classroom or separate school is justified only for students whose severity of disability along with the use of supplementary aids and services cannot be achieved satisfactorily in the general education environment (IDEA, 2004). However, Kart and Kart (2021) reported that in 2017, 95% of students with disabilities received an education in general education schools, and approximately 65% of students with disabilities who were in general education spent 80% or more time in general education classrooms. As such, general education teachers will be required to instruct students with disabilities. The assumption in keeping students with disabilities in the general education is to reduce the stigma of being segregated from their peers without disabilities.

Role of Special Education Teachers

Special education teachers serve a unique and essential role in the education of students with disabilities. Special education teachers have knowledge about how different disabilities can impact learning, and they have strategies to circumvent these academic and behavioral challenges. Because special education teachers have skills to modify instruction at the individual level, the unique needs of each student are addressed. Therefore, the likelihood that students will experience greater academic and behavioral success in the general education classroom increases. However, in circumstances where the student requires a different setting based on their individual needs, special education resource teachers can deliver specialized services to students in a separate resource classroom for part of the school day, depending on how much time the student needs to master the academic content.

Special education teachers are trained to have specific knowledge about the characteristics of students with disabilities. Special educators are the only professionals who have extensive preparation in teaching students with disabilities and are trained to know more about resources available to help students with disabilities (Strassfeld, 2019). An important role of special education teachers is to serve as facilitators (Holdheide & Reschly, 2008). In this role, special education teachers adapt instruction in the general education classroom that is presented by the general education teacher and facilitate learning for the student in the resource room where they make modifications for the student.

Special education teachers are prepared to deliver instruction in multiple settings, such as general education classrooms where students are taught by a general education teacher; in a resources classroom where students are taught for some time by a special education teacher; in a special education classroom where a special education teacher provides instruction to a group of students with either one disability or a variety of disabilities; a special education day school, a separate school for students with a variety of disabilities. As such, special educators are uniquely positioned to provide a free appropriate public education (FAPE) in a variety of settings. As a reminder, the FAPE provision of the IDEA, which states that students who qualify for special education services must have an individualized education program (IEP) that responds to their academic and behavioral characteristics and is provided at no cost to their families.

> *Special educators are uniquely positioned to provide a free appropriate public education (FAPE) in a variety of settings.*

Most students with disabilities are provided with instruction in regular public schools. Special educators teach only a small percentage (2.8%) of students with disabilities in a separate school. Another 2.2% of students with disabilities receive education in regular private schools, in separate residential facilities, at home, in a hospital, or in juvenile correctional facilities (Holdheide & Reschly, 2008). The fact that special education teachers spend most of their time providing support to students with disabilities in general education classrooms means that they will most likely be in a classroom sharing instructional space with a general education teacher. Therefore, collaboration is necessary.

Common Barriers That Limit Collaboration Between Educators

Collaboration has been defined as a professional partnership between two or more coequal educators who share responsibility, accountability, and resources (Da Fonte & Barton-Arwood, 2017). Many teacher preparation programs in the US are discrete programs. That means that special and general educators are in separate programs (Kaczorowski & Kline, 2018). Therefore, it is critical for general education and special education teachers to learn to communicate and collaborate with each other. Preparing teachers to collaborate effectively to teach students with disabilities takes effort, diligence, and training (Da Fonte & Barton-Arwood, 2017).

Lack of understanding about the roles and responsibilities of general education and special education teachers is a significant barrier to collaboration. General education teachers are responsible for developing and implementing an academic curriculum that responds to the state-level academic standards for a large group of students (Hansen et al., 2020). Elementary-level general education teachers typically are responsible for meeting a variety of academic standards (i.e., math, social studies, and English) at their respective grade levels for a group of about 20–30 students. Secondary school-level general education teachers typically teach one academic subject for 5 or 6 time periods during the school day to about 20–30 students per period. Therefore, secondary school-level teachers are responsible for ensuring that approximately 100 students meet subject-specific (e.g., math, social studies, English) academic standards.

> *Lack of understanding about the roles and responsibilities of general education and special education teachers is a significant barrier to collaboration.*

Typically, special education teachers have a caseload of approximately 22 students with disabilities, depending on the state in which they teach (Hogue & Taylor, 2020). Having 22 students with disabilities in different classrooms means that special education teachers must prepare that number of IEPs and maintain all the paperwork required to meet federal guidelines (Hogue & Taylor, 2020). Writing an IEP means that special education teachers will have different grade levels, different academic areas to cover, typically with limited knowledge of the content area. For example, special education teachers may or may not have postsecondary training in mathematics curriculum, yet they will need to adapt instruction for a student with a math disability. In sum, special education teachers have skills in making accommodations and modifications to allow students with disabilities to learn, and general education teachers are prepared to deliver academic instruction to typical students. However, general and special education teachers have limited understanding about what the other knows or is prepared to do (Da Fonte & Barton-Arwood, 2017).

IDEA and Parent Involvement

The IDEA considers parental involvement a necessary element for student success and gives parents or guardians considerable rights to participate in the educational process of their children with disabilities (Burke et al., 2021). Parental involvement has been a central goal in special education legislation since it was signed into law in 1975 (Strassfeld, 2019). According to Strassfeld (2019), school-level reports around the US show that parent and guardian participation ranges from a low of 20% to a high of 97%. The IDEA considers activities like communicating with school personnel, participating in decision-making, and advocating for their children as examples of parent participation. Since 1997, policy makers, through the IDEA, have charged schools to make greater efforts to increase parent involvement and increase the participation of general education teachers in the special education process for students with disabilities. However, in many cases, parent or guardian involvement in their child's education is commonly at odds with educators or it is one fraught with adversity with school administrators.

Common Barriers That Limit Collaboration Between Parents and Educators

Negative expectations are a common barrier to collaboration between parents or guardians and educators (Lauer, 2014). Many parents or guardians expect to have to fight with school personnel on behalf of their children with disabilities. It is common that parents or guardians feel that their voice is not heard or is disregarded by educators. In addition, parents or guardians believe they are at a disadvantage because they do not understand the process of special education and are unfamiliar with the educational terms. The field of special education has many acronyms and jargon which sounds foreign to anyone unfamiliar with them. For example, the sentence "IDEA requires schools to meet the FAPE provision through an IEP in the LRE" is understood by special education and many general educators, but it will likely mean nothing to a parent who is beginning to learn about the special education provisions offered to children with disabilities. Language and cultural differences may also limit collaboration between parents or guardians and educators. For example, if a parent does not speak or read English, they cannot respond to phone calls or written correspondence (Rogers-Adkinson et al., 2003). Parents or guardians might also view teachers as cold and uncaring for their child when they talk about numbers or test results, making it difficult for parents or guardians to see that teachers do care about their children. On the other hand, teachers may also hold negative views of parents or guardians. For example, teachers often assume a lack of interest in their children when parents or guardians do not respond to telephone or written correspondence. In addition, teachers may view a parent as uncaring if parents or guardians do not attend meetings for their child. In contrast, teachers may view parents or guardians as aggressive when they express disagreement with a decision taken by the teacher. These bidirectional negative views between parents or guardians and educators often result in an antagonistic relationship between parents or guardians.

Another often unrecognized barrier to collaboration between parents or guardians and teachers is the type of communication teachers have with parents or guardians. Most communication with parents or guardians of children with disabilities is characterized as bad news. Teachers generally communicate with parents or guardians to tell them that their child is not doing well in academics or behaviorally. The phone call home is seldom one in which the teacher is calling with news that the student completed his or her homework or understood the mathematical concepts. For the most part, teachers tend to call home when something is wrong. When parents or guardians of children with disabilities get phone calls from the teacher or school, those calls tend to be about the behavior of their children, telling them that their child is in trouble. These phone calls create tension between the parents or guardians and school and put added strain on the family's ability to care for their children with disabilities (Brannan, 2003). Awareness of barriers to collaboration and a genuine effort to engage parents or guardians of students with disabilities in the educational process of their children will likely minimize the likelihood that parents or guardians will file complaints through the procedural safeguards or due process available to them in the IDEA. In the final section of this chapter, we offer suggestions to work successfully with parents or guardians of students with disabilities.

Suggestions for Successful Collaboration and Partnerships Between Educators and Parents

It is important to understand that participation, involvement, engagement, and collaboration are related terms, yet there are subtle but significant differences between them. *Participation* means to take action. Someone who participates will attend meetings, fill out paperwork, and comply with the basic requirements expected of them. *Involvement* means that someone is doing something to another person. Someone who is involved is having something done to them, according to Ferlazzo (2011). Ferlazzo (2011) defines *engagement* as a combination of participation (or action) with commitment or investment in what they are doing. Finally, *collaboration* is defined as action taken by individuals of equal status with a same goal. Thus, while the IDEA stresses parent participation and involvement, it is important that teachers seek collaboration between themselves and with parents or guardians to form partnerships on behalf of each student with disabilities. To build strong and effective partnerships, it is important for each partner to understand the important and critical nature of their role in the education of students with disabilities and to recognize the preconceived biases and inaccurate perceptions they may have of each other.

Teachers must recognize that parents or guardians are experts on their children (Burke et al., 2021). Parents or guardians and general educators must recognize that special educators are experts on knowledge about special education law, characteristics of students with disabilities, and special education teaching strategies (Holdheide & Reschly, 2008). General education teachers are experts on general education curriculum and state-level standards (Holdheide & Reschly, 2008). This section focuses on strategies that can increase collaboration between general educators, special educators, and parents or guardians.

The idea that parents or guardians must fight with school personnel to meet the needs of their child with a disability is erroneous (Lauer, 2014). The groundbreaking cases (e.g., *Endrew F. v. Douglas County School District*) discussed in Chapter 2 are examples of instances in which the parents or guardians of children with disabilities had to seek legal interference to meet their child's needs in school. However, most schools desire the opportunity to work with parents or guardians instead of seeking legal action when there are disagreements. The first suggestion to improve collaboration is to dispel the misunderstanding that parents or guardians and teachers are adversaries. Lauer (2014) describes a mother's surprise when she realized during her first meeting with the school's team that each person on the team was willing to work with her to meet the needs of her autistic son. She was delighted that they read the reports she generated with other professionals outside the school and that the members of the school's team were willing to implement the recommendations within the reports. The mother was prepared to advocate for her son against the school team, but she found that the school team was working with her in the best interest of her son. This example is one type of parent–school collaboration which shows that parents or guardians and the school can work together to advocate on behalf of children with disabilities (Ferlazzo, 2011).

Teachers might begin meetings with a parent by reminding parents or guardians that the school is a partner in the education of students with disabilities, thereby defusing a parent's fear that the interaction with the school will be antagonistic. Teachers can increase parent engagement by being explicit about what the teacher wants the parent to do. For example, in some instances, teachers only want the parent to help them with the basic task of ensuring that the student completes their homework. In this case, the teacher might communicate that a checkmark indicating homework completion is all the teacher is looking for from the parent. It is also important for the teacher and school not to blame the parents or guardians for their children's disability. Parents or guardians might already be experiencing feelings of guilt and shame due to their child's learning challenges.

In cases where general or special education teachers need more from parents or guardians, it is important to communicate clearly with parents or guardians and offer them a way to prepare for the meeting. For example, if the reason for a meeting is to discuss placement options, teachers can discuss potential options that may be considered and what each option entails. This helps parents or guardians prepare adequately for the meeting and be able to contribute meaningfully during the meeting. In meetings that are at the start of parents' experience with special education, special education teachers should send home a list of terms and their acronyms with a copy of the parental rights, to allow the parent to become familiar with the many terms used in the meeting. In cases where the parents or guardians are employed and need to take off time from work, the school might also provide information about how the Family Medical Leave Act could allow them to take time off work to attend IEP meetings related to their children with disabilities. It is also important for teachers and the school to remember that while some parents or guardians have the possibility of rescheduling their workday, other parents or guardians do not. Thus, for parents or guardians who have jobs that are less flexible, parental participation may be more likely if meetings are scheduled outside of the parent's workday.

Another way of increasing parent collaboration is to communicate with the parents or guardians when things are going well in the school with their child. All too often, teachers communicate with parents or guardians only when students with disabilities are experiencing difficulties (Carlson et al., 2020). Finding opportunities to share successes that the student with disabilities is achieving in the classroom might balance out the other times when teachers need to call home with bad news or a problem. While it is important to communicate to parents or guardians concerns about their child, it is also important to reach out to parents or guardians when things are going well in the classroom. Table 5.1 provides suggestions for how general education teachers can share good news to parents or guardians of children with disabilities. Sending an email that the parent can read at a time it is convenient for them might be the way to start sharing good news with parents or guardians.

TABLE 5.1 Suggestions for Communicating Good News to Parents of Children with Disabilities

Form of Communication	Example
Email	Dear Ms. Patterson, I have good news to share about your son Jason. This week he successfully submitted his homework 4 out of 5 days. I appreciate the support you are providing at home, and I look forward to our continued collaboration to help him maintain his accomplishment or increase it to the full five days. I told Jason I would be sending you this information. Please congratulate him on this great accomplishment and let him know we are both proud of him for focusing on improving his homework submission.
Phone Call	Great news, Ms. Patterson, Jason successfully submitted his homework this week. I was hoping to talk to you in person, but it looks like you are busy being a great mom. Please accept my personal thanks for partnering with me to help Jason submit his homework. If you have time, send me an email or return my call so I know you received this message where I am bragging to you about Jason.

When sending an electronic message to a parent, make sure the email subject line is something that conveys good news immediately. Similarly, phone messages should begin immediately with good news, as in the example in Table 5.1. Because parents or guardians of students with disabilities might anticipate that a general education teacher only contacts them with bad news about their child, teachers need to help parents or guardians find reasons to feel proud of their children. Many parents or guardians of students with disabilities mostly have experienced challenges and obstacles in school. Knowing when things are going well will allow parents or guardians to celebrate accomplishments while staying focused on the ongoing work and effort required to raise a child with a disability.

One way to communicate with parents or guardians of students with disabilities is through daily home journals. Teachers can write a note in the journal, which the student takes home to show the parents or guardians. In this home journal, teachers can praise and thank the parent for their ongoing efforts at home to help the student with his or her homework. The combination of concerns and praise allows parents or guardians to feel that their work at home is valued by the teacher. Another way that teachers might consider approaching parents or guardians when there is trouble with the student is to state what is going on at school and ask the parent if something similar is going on at home. Asking questions allows the parent to reflect on potential changes in the home environment without the sting of feeling accused by the teacher. Empathy for the stress experienced by many parents or guardians of children with disabilities might help teachers treat parents or guardians with kindness and understanding. Table 5.2 is a checklist teachers can use to communicate more empathically with parents or guardians.

TABLE 5.2 Parent Communication Checklist

Questions to Consider Before a Meeting with Parents or Guardians of Children with Disabilities	Example of Content of the Letter
Is my message to parents or guardians clear about the reason for the meeting?	We would like to meet with you to go over the results of the educational evaluation the IEP team conducted.
Did I give parents or guardians options for the date and time of the meeting?	The IEP team can meet with you in the afternoons in case you need to work around your job schedule. We have scheduled the meeting for April 20, 2023, from 5 to 6 p.m. If the day and time we offered is not possible, please give us a day and time that is better suited for you to attend the meeting.
Is the tone of the language friendly and reassuring?	I realize this is your first meeting about your son's learning difficulties, and I imagine you might feel unsure of what to expect. I want to let you know that I will sit next to you in case you have questions for me during the meeting. As his teacher, I am on your side to figure out how to help Tim.
Did I ask the parent if they need a translator?	The meeting will be in English. I can invite a translator, or you can bring your own if you wish if you prefer a language other than English.
Did you invite the parent to contact you if something is unclear or there are questions?	I look forward to seeing you. Please feel free to call me at (812) 555-2802 or email me at teacher@school.gov if you have any questions prior to the meeting.

Suggestions to Improve Collaboration Between General and Special Educators

Collaboration between special education and general education teachers can take two forms: direct and indirect, according to Hansen et al. (2020). **Direct collaboration** means that the special education teacher, who has specialized knowledge and techniques about disabilities, provides direct instructional support to the student with disabilities in or outside the general education classroom (Hansen et al., 2020). In direct collaboration, the special education teacher instructs one student or several students with disabilities in the general education classroom while the general educator teaches the other students in the classroom. In other words, in direct collaboration, the special educator teaches the student with disabilities. **Indirect collaboration** involves the special education teacher providing support to the general education teacher, who in turn works with the student with disabilities. In this form of collaboration, the special education teacher provides tips for the general education teacher to implement with the student with disabilities and the other students in the classroom. According to Hansen et al. (2020), the goal of indirect collaboration is for the general education teacher to have access to the special educator's knowledge and experience helping all students in the classroom, not only the few students with disabilities. Regardless of which form of collaboration is used, it is important for both general and special education teachers to communicate explicitly about which form of collaboration they engage in to minimize misunderstandings or conflict between them.

Insufficient time to plan together is a major barrier to collaboration between general and special education teachers (Da Fonte & Barton-Arwood, 2017). Both special education and general education teachers have a significant amount of work to do during the school day, but it is imperative to find time to plan together. Because time is limited, it is important to arrive on time and be prepared, stay focused on the student's needs, and minimize distractions. While it is important for general and special education teachers to find time to build rapport with one another, the planning period should be for working on the student's academic and behavioral needs rather than time for teachers to get to know one another (Da Fonte & Barton-Arwood, 2017).

Summary

Collaboration among general and special education teachers and parents or guardians is essential to maximize the learning success of students with disabilities. While it is inevitable that disagreements might arise, understanding the role each educator plays in the education of students with disabilities will increase the likelihood that the IDEA's expectations of collaboration will be met. When disagreements do arise, communicating directly and clearly with one another and giving each other the benefit of the doubt will minimize friction between educators and parents or guardians to allow the IEP team to stay focused on the academic and behavioral goals of students with disabilities.

Test Your Knowledge

1. What are common barriers to collaboration between parents or guardians and teachers of students with disabilities?
2. How is collaboration different from engagement, involvement, and participation?
3. What are the different roles parents or guardians, general education teachers, and special education teachers have in the education of students with disabilities?
4. Why is it important to understand the unique role each educator plays in the education of students with disabilities?

Apply Your Knowledge

Revisit the *Rowley* and *Endrew* cases in Chapter 2. In each case, consider what may have transpired leading parents or guardians to activate the procedural safeguard (or due process) provision of the IDEA.

Ask

Ask yourself the following question to help guide your reading.

- If you were Amy's or Endrew's teacher, what would you do differently to collaborate with parents or guardians?

Read

Read the following sections.

- *Rowley* Case (p. 15)
- *Endrew* Case (p. 16)
- IDEA and Parent Involvement (p. 54)
- Common Barriers That Limit Collaboration Between Parents or Guardians and Educators (p. 54)
- Table 5.2 Parent Communication Checklist (p. 58)

Tell

Tell your response.

Respond to the following and remember to use professional language and to show empathy and support toward parents or guardians:

- What are potential roadblocks that can arise by not involving parents or guardians in the collaborative process of their child's special education process?
- Write a letter to Amy's parents or guardians in response to their desire for their daughter to have a sign language interpreter be included in her IEP provisions.
- Write a letter to Endrew's parents or guardians in response to their concern about their child not making progress toward his academic goals because your curriculum is insufficiently challenging.

References

Brannan, A. M. (2003). Ensuring effective mental health treatment in real-world settings and the critical role of families. *Journal of Child & Family Studies, 12*(1), 1–10. https://doi.org/10.1023/A:1021385223674

Burke, M. M., Rossetti, Z., Aleman-Tovar, J., Rios, K., Lee, J., Schraml-Block, K., & Rivera, J. (2021). Comparing special education experiences among Spanish- and English-speaking parents of children with disabilities. *Journal of Developmental and Physical Disabilities, 33*:117–135.

Carlson, R. G., Hock, R., George, M., Kumpiene, G., Yell, M., McCartney, E. D., Riddle, D., & Weist, M. D. (2020). Relational factors influencing parents' engagement in special education for high school youth with emotional/behavioral problems. *Behavioral Disorders 45*(2) 103–116.

Christopulos, T. T., & Kean, J. (2020). General education teachers' contribution to the identification of children with language disorders. *Perspectives of the ASHA Special Interest Groups, 5,* 770–777.

Da Fonte, M. A., & Barton-Arwood, S. M. (2017). Collaboration of general and special education teachers: Perspectives and strategies. *Intervention in School and Clinic, 53*(2) 99–106.

Ferlazzo, L. (May 2011). Involvement or engagement? *Educational Leadership,* 10–14.

Hansen, J. H., Carrington, S., Jensen, C. R., Molbæk, M., & Schmidt, M. C. S. (2020) The collaborative practice of inclusion and exclusion. *Nordic Journal of Studies in Educational Policy, 6*(1), 47–57. doi:10.1080/20020317.2020.1730112

Hogue, L. B., & Taylor, S. S. (2020). A review of special education caseload policies state by state: What impact do they have? *Journal of Special Education Leadership, 33*(1), 1–11.

Holdheide, L. R., & Reschly, D. J. (2008). Teacher preparation to deliver inclusive services to students with disabilities: TQ connection issue paper. In *National Comprehensive Center for Teacher Quality.* National Comprehensive Center for Teacher Quality.

Individuals with Disabilities Education Improvement Act of 2004, Pub. L. No. 108-446, 118 Stat. 2647 (2004).

Kaczorowski, T., & Kline, S. M. (2018). Teachers' perceptions of preparedness to teach students with disabilities. *Mid-Western Educational Researcher, 33*(1), 36–58.

Kart, A., & Kart, M. (2021). Academic and social effects of inclusion on students without disabilities: A review of the literature. *Education Sciences, 11*(1), 16.

Lauer, V. K. (2014). *When the school says no ... How to get the yes! Securing special education services for your child.* Jessica Kingsley Publishers.

Ochoa, T. A. (2018). Bilingual special education. In C. J. Ovando and M. C. Combs (Eds.), *Bilingual and ESL classrooms* (6th ed., pp. 345–369). Rowman & Littlefield.

Rogers-Adkinson, D., Ochoa, T. A., & Delgado, B. (2003). Developing cross cultural competence in serving families with children with significant developmental needs. *Journal of Autism and Developmental Disorders, 18,* 4–8.

Strassfeld, N. M. (2019). Preparing pre-service special education teachers to facilitate parent involvement, knowledge, and advocacy: Considerations for curriculum. *Teacher Education and Special Education, 42*(4) 283–296.

Characteristics and Needs of Students with High-Incidence Disabilities

6

This chapter provides information about the academic, social-emotional, and behavioral needs of students with disabilities. This is particularly important to general education teachers, since 64% of students with high-incidence disabilities, as discussed in Chapter 4, spend 80% or more of the day in the general education setting.

In this chapter, readers will:

- Learn which 7 of the 13 categories in the IDEA are considered high-incidence disabilities;
- Develop an understanding of the academic, social-emotional, and behavioral needs of students with high-incidence disabilities;
- Define **inclusive education**;
- Gain insight on the range of the abilities and needs among students with high-incidence disabilities.

After reading this chapter, readers will:

- Discuss the range of academic, social-emotional, and behavioral needs of students with disabilities;
- Identify relevant accommodations that can be implemented in general education classrooms to support specific student needs.

All Future Educators
Special education goes beyond academic instruction and support. Student social-emotional and behavioral needs should also be addressed.

Elementary General Education
Elementary school teachers, especially those in primary (K-2), are essential for partners in providing early intervention services to prevent future learning loss for school-aged children.

Secondary General Education
Secondary school teachers begin preparing students formally for transition out of school and into adult life. They can help collaborate with special educators to develop supports within their content area to help students meet their transition goals.

Special Education
Special educators receive more comprehensive training on the characteristics of students with disabilities. They can help general educators, as well as administrators, understand their students better.

Undergraduates Interested in Disability Laws
The IDEA provides a general outline of what each special education category must include; however, the law can be vague, and individual states or districts may interpret the law differently.

Supporting Students with Disabilities in School

According to the National Center for Education Statistics (NCES, 2020), approximately 7.1 million students between the ages of 3–21 in public schools, or 14% of the total student population, received special education services in 2018–2019. **The inclusive education** reform movement, discussed briefly in Chapter 2 (full inclusion versus partial inclusion), promotes the idea that, to the extent possible, students with disabilities should be educated along with their non-disabled peers. Chapter 6 is intended to provide information about the characteristics of students with high-incidence disabilities as general education teachers will likely have students with high-incidence disabilities in their classrooms.

As discussed in Chapter 3, the Individuals with Disabilities Education Improvement Act (IDEA) mandates schools to provide an individualized education program (IEP) and special education services to students with disabilities when their disability impedes learning. The IDEA recognizes 13 categories of disabilities under which students can receive special education services. As discussed in Chapter 4, seven of the categories of disability among the list of 13 recognized by the IDEA are more common than others. In addition, students with disabilities or disorders who are not eligible for special education can receive support through 504 plans to improve academic skills, as well as social-emotional and behavioral skills related to a variety of medical and other health conditions. According to the National Center on Education Outcomes (NCEO, 2016), accurate counts of students with 504 plans are not available; however, some estimates report less than 1% of the school-aged population nationally.

High-Incidence Categories of Disabilities Recognized in the IDEA

The most common category of disability among students served under the IDEA is the category of specific learning disability (SLD). Data provided by the NCES (2020) indicated that 33% of all students identified as having a disability under the IDEA were identified as having an SLD. As indicated in Figure 6.1, 19% of all identified disabilities were speech impairment (SI) or language impairment, also referred to as communication disorders. Other health impairment (OHI) and autism spectrum disorder were identified in 15% and 11%, respectively. Additionally, 7% of students receiving special education did so for developmental delay (DD) and 6% for intellectual disability (ID). The smallest category of disability under the IDEA discussed in this chapter was emotional disturbance (5%). It should be noted that the term *emotional disturbance*, used in the IDEA, is out of favor with most scholars and practitioners. The term emotional and behaviors disorder (EBD) is preferred over emotional disturbance. In the following sections, we discuss the academic, social-emotional, and behavioral characteristics and needs of students with disabilities.

Students with Specific Learning Disabilities

As nearly one-third of all students with disabilities will be identified as having a specific learning disability, it is important for general education teachers to know how specific learning disabilities

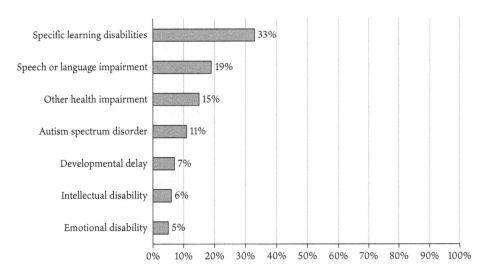

FIGURE 6.1 High-incidence disabilities in public schools

may manifest and to know how to support students with specific learning disabilities in the general education classroom. For example, students with reading disabilities related to reading fluency may require additional time on related tasks (e.g., in-class assignments, homework, or assessments), or may require items read aloud.

IDEA Category and Criteria

According to the IDEA, students with specific learning disabilities (SLD) have an impairment in one or more of their basic psychological functions, or cognitive functions, which impedes their ability to process information. This can manifest as an "imperfect ability to listen, speak, read, write, spell, or do mathematical calculations" (IDEA, Sec. 300.8). Specific learning disabilities are not primarily a result of visual, hearing, or motor (fine or gross) abilities, or due to an intellectual disability, or an emotional disorder. Additionally, specific learning disabilities are not due to environmental, cultural, or economic disadvantage.

Academic Needs

Impairments in one or more psychological, or cognitive, abilities may negatively affect how students understand or process information and may negatively affect student performance in one or more areas of achievement. These include reading, mathematics, written expression, oral expression, or listening comprehension. A limitation, or impairment, in one area of psychological or cognitive ability may also manifest in one or more areas of academic achievement. For example, students who experience difficulty in reading comprehension may also experience difficulty in listening comprehension or other language-related areas.

> *Impairments in one or more psychological, or cognitive, abilities may negatively affect how students understand or process information and may negatively affect student performance in one or more area of achievement.*

Students may have a specific learning disability in one or more areas of academic functioning, depending on the area of psychological, or cognitive, weaknesses and strengths. The five main categories of specific learning disabilities are presented below.

- **Reading.** One or more areas related to reading: basic reading skills, reading fluency, and reading comprehension.
- **Mathematics.** One or more areas related to mathematics: mathematics calculation and mathematics problem solving,
- **Written Expression.** Written expression involves the integration of oral language, written language, overall cognitive (psychological ability), and motor skills. Written expression may involve one or more of the following: handwriting, spelling, and the content of writing (grammar, structure, etc.).
- **Oral Expression.** Includes expressive or spoken language (being understood by others) and may manifest in reading, writing, spelling, or mathematics.
- **Listening Comprehension.** Includes receptive or oral language (understanding others) and may manifest in reading, writing, spelling, or mathematics. Students with listening comprehension disabilities may struggle to follow oral directions.

Social-Emotional and Behavioral Needs

Students with specific learning disabilities experience complex challenges which may impact their overall information processing and language expression skills. This would also impact how they communicate with others, including their peers. Students with specific learning disabilities report lower ratings in self-esteem at school and engaged in more maladaptive strategies than their general education peers (Alesi et al., 2012). Parents of students with learning disorders also report higher incidents of anxiety and depression in their children with specific learning disabilities compared to parents of children without specific learning disabilities. Students with specific learning disabilities may also procrastinate, put less effort into their work, and avoid challenging situations as a way to avoid feelings of inadequacy. Interventions which focus on academic skill attainment, organizational learning strategies, and adaptive strategies, including strategies that encourage self-advocacy, may help to address the academic, social-emotional, and behavioral needs to students with specific learning disabilities.

Students with Speech or Language Impairments

Approximately 19% of students with disabilities served under the IDEA were students with speech impairment or language impairment, which fall under the broader category of communication disorders. It is important for general education teachers to understand how a communication disorder may be exhibited, as well as how to support students with communication disorders in the general education classroom. Because so much classroom instruction is based in communication, or language (written, spoken, nonverbal), students with communication disorders may need support understanding instructions, expressing their understanding, or with understanding the nonverbal parts of communication, such as recognizing and understanding body language.

IDEA Category and Criteria

According to the American Speech-Language-Hearing Association (ASHA, 1993), a communication disorder is defined as an impairment in the processes of hearing, language, and/or speech that affects the ability to understand, receive, send, or process verbal or nonverbal language. In the IDEA (2004), students with communication disorders may receive services under the category of speech impairments (**SI**) or language impairments (**LI**). *Speech* refers to articulation of speech sounds, fluency, and voice quality. *Language* refers to the content, form, and function of language, as well as the nonverbal social aspects of language.

Academic Needs

Students with speech impairments (SI) may be provided with support from direct services from a speech and language pathologist (SLP), as well as through their general education teachers through consultation with an SLP. Direct services refers to services provided directly from a paraprofessional, such as an SLP. Indirect, or consultative, services are those wherein the paraprofessional does not work directly with the student, but rather provides training to individuals, such as teachers, who will be working directly with the students. Speech services include those that address (ASHA, 1993):

- Articulation or sound production (substitution, omitting, adding, or distorting certain speech sounds);
- Speech fluency (rate, rhythm, and repletion of sounds); and
- Voice (quality, pitch, and volume).

Like with speech impairments, students with language impairments (LI) may be provided with direct support from an SLP or through their general education teachers, through consultation with an SLP. Language services include those that address (ASHA, 1993):

- The formation of language (sounds combinations, structure, and order);
- The content of language (meaning); and
- The function of language (integration of language and socially appropriate communication).

Social-Emotional and Behavioral Needs

Students with communication disorders who experience difficulties expressing their wants, needs, and ideas may also develop difficulty expressing their emotions, which in turn may adversely impact their social skills, including interpersonal relationships with peers and adults, self-image, self-control, social interactions, and social understanding (Gregg, 2017). Students with communication disorders may demonstrate aggressive behavior or social withdrawal. Adults responsible for educating and caring for students with communication disorders may also become frustrated when they are unable to understand the child's needs or when the child uses aggression or withdrawal to communicate their emotions. Just as those maladaptive behaviors affect the child's peer relationships, they also can impact the relationship or connection a student has with the adult (Gregg, 2017). These maladaptive behaviors manifested by students with communication disorders may serve three main functions: to escape or avoid a non-preferred activity or environment, to gain something such as a tangible object (toy or other item) or control of the situation, or to get attention from peers or adults (Gregg, 2017). Interventions that focus on alternative or simplified means of communication may help to support social-emotional and behavioral needs of students with communication disorders and they may also reinforce more appropriate communication skills.

Students with Other Health Impairments

Fifteen percent of students with disabilities are identified with other health impairments based on the IDEA criteria. Students with health impairments that negatively impact their ability to attend to relevant stimuli (instruction, schoolwork, classroom projects, etc.) may experience academic needs across various subjects. Attention deficit hyperactivity disorder (ADHD) is a common condition identified and served under the OHI category of the IDEA. As discussed previously in this chapter, not all students with medical diagnoses, such as ADHD, are eligible for special education. To qualify for special education services under the IDEA, an adverse educational impact needs to be evidenced and related to the other health impairment.

IDEA Category and Criteria

The IDEA defines other health impairments (OHI) as conditions that limit "strength, vitality, or alertness, including a heightened alertness to environmental stimuli" (IDEA, Sec. 300.8). This is exhibited as a difficulty sustaining attention and focus, and negatively impacts educational performance. As discussed above, the most common health problem covered by OHI is attention deficit hyperactivity disorder (ADHD); according to the IDEA, other disorders which may impact school performance, focus, and attention include, but are not limited to, asthma, diabetes, heart conditions, lead poisoning, leukemia and other cancers, sickle cell anemia, and Tourette syndrome.

Academic Needs

When students are unable to sustain attention to relevant stimuli during instruction, they may require special education services and support across various subjects (reading, mathematics, science, social studies). For students with OHI, academic concerns most often arise in elementary school and continue through college (DuPaul et al., 2016). For students with OHI—specifically with ADHD—executive function skills, such as attentiveness, task persistence, eagerness to learn, learning independently, task organization, and flexibility, were lower (DuPaul et al., 2016). Executive functioning skills are the more integrative and complex processes involved in starting, sustaining focus on, and completing academic work.

Social-Emotional and Behavioral Needs

Students who experience difficulty sustaining attention and focus may also demonstrate significant impairments in interpersonal skills, including initiating and maintaining friendships, getting along with others who are different, showing empathy or helping other children, and expressing themselves in positive ways (DuPaul et al., 2016). Students with other health impairments, especially those with ADHD, may also demonstrate hyperactive or impulsive behaviors. Hyperactivity and impulsivity in childhood significantly contribute to inattentiveness in early adolescence (Greven et al., 2011). Early interventions that focus on hyperactive or impulsive behaviors, such as redirecting hyperactive behaviors; creating structure for initiating, sustaining focus on, and completing tasks; and other executive functions may help to support academic, social-emotional, and behavioral needs.

Students with Autism Spectrum Disorder

The population of individuals with autism spectrum disorder (**ASD**) is increasing. Myers et al. (2018) reported that 1 out of 142 individuals meet criteria for ASD. Pop culture popularized the idea that people with ASD, such as Temple Grandin, are accomplished and even gifted. However, this is not always the case. Individuals with ASD may have what is referred to as autistic savant syndrome, which is defined as having an extreme talent such as a photographic memory (the ability to memorize and recall a phone book page by simply looking at it); however, these individuals are rare (Hallahan et al., 2019) and would require significant support in all other areas of academic, social-emotional, and behavioral functioning. Students with ASD often require more intensive instruction and supports in a more restrictive setting, such as self-contained classrooms. However, students with ASD may also be in general education classrooms. Thus, it is important for general education teachers to understand the characteristics of students with ASD to ensure that they receive sustained academic and behavioral support.

IDEA Category and Criteria

The IDEA defines autism in Section 300.8 as a developmental disability that significantly affects verbal and nonverbal communication and social interactions. Other characteristics typically demonstrated by students with autism include engaging in repetitive and restrictive behaviors, exhibiting resistance to changes in daily routines, and having unusual negative responses to sensory stimulation. ASD is generally evident before the age of three. As with other health impairment, to qualify for services under the IDEA, the disability must have an adverse effect on a student's educational performance.

Academic Needs

The academic needs of students with ASD will vary depending on their level of intellectual abilities. While some students with ASD have intelligence quotient (IQ) levels beyond (standard score of 85–100) or above the average (standard score >100) range, many other students with ASD have intellectual disabilities (IQ less than standard score of 70). Students with autism may require instructional support, such as instruction provided at a quick pace and paired with a reinforcement (a reward) as soon as the student engages in the desired behavior (MacDonald et al., 2018). These two elements are believed to help the student acquire new academic skills. Additionally, students with ASD often require support with language skills to communicate with the teacher or classroom peers. Students with ASD may also need social skills instruction, since they may have difficulties interpreting social cues or the hidden curriculum because they lack the ability to understand and decode nonverbal behavior.

Social-Emotional and Behavioral Needs

Social-emotional and behavioral needs range in severity between individuals with ASD. Students with ASD demonstrate deficits in social communication and interactions (American Psychological Association [APA], 2013), including difficulty with typical back-and-forth conversation, abnormal social approach, as well as poorly integrated verbal and nonverbal skills, including appropriate and congruent facial expressions and affect. Additionally, students with ASD experience difficulties developing, understanding, and maintaining interpersonal relationships (APA, 2013). Another feature of ASD is a restrictive or repetitive pattern of behaviors or interests (APA, 2013). This may include the use of stereotypy behavior (lining up toys, flipping objects), echolalia (repetition of vocalizations of another person), and idiosyncratic phrases (words of phrase used in an irrelevant or unrelated way), rigid adherence to routines or schedules, fixated interests that appear overly intense or focused, and an over- or under-sensitivity to sensory stimuli (clothing or food textures, sound, pain tolerance, temperature, excessive smelling of objects). Social stories are useful tools to teach students with ASD the nuances of interpersonal interactions and behavioral functioning. Additionally, the Picture Exchange Communication System (PECS) is useful to help students with significant communication skills and is a way to make their needs known through pictures and words.

Students with Developmental Delay

According to the IDEA, students with developmental delay fall between the ages of 3–9; however, the maximum age may vary state to state, but will not exceed age 9. It is important for elementary school teachers who teach children younger than 9 years of age to understand the characteristics of students with developmental delays, since early interventions to ameliorate these developmental delays can be provided before the child enters school.

IDEA Category and Criteria

As outlined above, developmental delays (**DD**), as described in Section 300.8 of the IDEA, refers to children under the age of 9 years of age who have not reached expected developmental milestones in the typical process of childhood development. *Developmental milestones* relates to the physical development (fine or gross motor), intellectual or cognitive development, communication skills, social or emotional skills, or adaptive behaviors compared to children of similar age (IDEA, 2004). In most instances of developmental delays, the cause is unknown. Parents (or primary caregivers) are commonly a primary source of reporting delays in reaching developmental milestones because they spend the majority of time with children.

Academic, Social-Emotional, and Behavioral Needs

Students with DD may demonstrate intellectual, communication, behavioral, or social problems. Early intervention specific to the aspect of delay is crucial to minimize the exacerbation of those needs. Academic achievement is not explicitly discussed because many children are identified with DD prior to any formal school experience. When children with DD continue to demonstrate academic, social-emotional, or behavioral needs when they reach the maximum age (age 9 federally), they are reevaluated to determine if services are needed under a different special education category. Schools provide relevant services to help support students with DD from licensed individuals and personnel. Children with gross motor developmental delays may need physical therapy. Children with fine motor movement delays may need occupational therapy. Children with language production or comprehension problems need speech and language therapy. Children with social or emotional delays may need social-emotional learning interventions. Finally, children with delays in adaptive behaviors may need supports and services from both special education and general education teachers.

Students with Intellectual Disabilities

General education teachers are mostly likely to be familiar with students with one form of intellectual disability (**ID**) called Down syndrome since, according to Hallahan et al. (2019), Down syndrome is a common form of a genetic intellectual disability (ID). There are other IDs with known genetic causes such as Prader-Willi syndrome and Williams syndrome (Hallahan et al., 2019). However, not all IDs have a known genetic cause. Students with ID may have difficulties with reasoning, judgment, abstract thinking, problem solving, memory, learning from experience, and adaptive functioning (Tafla et al., 2021); however, it is important for general educators to understand that all students with ID can learn, even if they learn at a slower pace, compared to their peers without IDs.

IDEA Category and Criteria

The criteria for an intellectual disability under the IDEA stipulates a score of 70 or below as measured by an intelligence test such as the Woodcock-Johnson Tests of Cognitive Abilities or the Wechsler Intelligence Scale for Children. In the IDEA, there are four subcategories of IDs: mild (IQ standard score between 69 to 55); moderate (IQ standard score between 54–40); severe (IQ standard score between 39–25); and profound (IQ standard score 24 or below). The 2019 National Survey of Children's Health estimated that 1.1% of students between the ages of 12 to 17 have an intellectual disability. Because there is variation in the levels of ID, the educational needs of students with ID vary.

Academic Needs

While some students with mild ID may be able to benefit from the general education curriculum across content areas, students with moderate and severe intellectual impairments may benefit from a functional curriculum. A functional curriculum may allow students with ID to learn skills needed to function in daily life (Doyle & Giangreco, 2013). A functional curriculum focuses on life skills to develop independence. The functional curriculum might focus on mathematical instruction to teach the student to count money. Functional reading may focus on teaching the student with ID to read a bus schedule. Students with mild ID might need step-by-step directions, concrete examples, and repetition to acquire academic concepts such as counting, reading, and writing.

Social-Emotional and Behavioral Needs

In terms of social skills, students with ID may need support with interpersonal skills, self-esteem, following the rules and laws, avoiding being victimized, and social problem solving (Tassé et al., 2012). Some students with ID need assistance, particularly as they enter adolescence if they also are overly trusting and gullible because they may be taken advantage of by their peers or coerced into engaging in inappropriate behaviors (Leffert et al., 2010). Students with ID may not engage in behaviors which are developmentally appropriate for their age (Tassé et al., 2012), may develop learned helplessness (sense of powerlessness caused by repeated failure to succeed), and may engage in task-avoidant behavior or display a lack of initiative (Gacek et al., 2017). Students with ID may need assistance in developing self-initiative to minimize their dependence on others. In addition to providing support for basic skills, such as counting, functional instruction benefits students with ID by increasing their independence in practical and self-care skills, such as taking the bus to work and grocery shopping.

Students with Emotional Disturbance

The category which may be most important for general education teachers to understand is the category of emotional disturbance (**ED**), also referred to as emotional and behavioral disability (**EBD**) or emotional disability. As discussed in Chapter 1, students with EBD or ED are at an increased risk for entering the school-to-prison pipeline compared to all other students with disabilities. Teachers who understand this category of disability can see students' classroom misbehavior as manifestation of the students' social-emotional needs.

IDEA Category and Criteria

The definition of ED includes internalizing (emotional) and externalizing (behavioral) dimensions. The criteria for ED say that students must show one or more of the following characteristics: an inability to form and maintain positive interpersonal relationships with peers or teachers, a general and pervasive mood of unhappiness or depression, fears associated with school or inappropriate types of feelings under normal circumstances, or schizophrenia. Most scholars prefer the term EBD rather than ED, the term used in the IDEA. The term EBD is used in the educational research because it is thought to capture the behavioral aspects of the disability, which *emotional disturbance* does not. For these reasons, we use the term EBD to refer to the IDEA's ED.

Conduct disorder (**CD**) is a common example of an externalizing EBD, while anxiety and depression are common examples of internalizing conditions of EBD (Oldenhof et al., 2020). Conservative estimates indicate that at least 2% of the entire school population show characteristics that would qualify them for services under the IDEA's criteria, yet less than 1% of students with such characteristics are identified as having EBD. Forness et al. (2012) have pointed out that using a psychiatric diagnosis would identify more children with moderate and severe forms of EBD. While identifying more children with EBD may appear counterintuitive, Forness et al. suggest that early identification would lead to better outcomes for these students because they will lead to early and more appropriate interventions for their disability.

Academic Needs

Students with EBD need academic instruction commensurate with their intellectual skills. While some students with EBD have average or above-average intelligence, others may have below average IQs, and many students with EBD have broad academic deficits (Garwood et al., 2021). As such, students with EBD may need academic instruction in math, reading, writing, and spelling. Additionally, subjects like social studies may help not only with academics but also provide instruction in civic education, which teaches students their rights and responsibilities toward others.

Social-Emotional and Behavioral Needs

Social-emotional needs refers to the internalizing components, or the emotional components, of EBD. The most common internalizing symptoms of EBD are anxiety and depression (Hallahan, Kauffman, & Pullen, 2019). Students may feel pervasive feelings of unhappiness or depression and feelings that are incongruent with the situation. One main feature of students with EBD, as defined by the IDEA (2004), is the inability to sustain interpersonal relationships with peers and adults. Garwood and his colleagues suggest that social skills instruction is an important need for students with EBD.

> *One main feature of students with EBD ... is the inability to sustain interpersonal relationships with peers and adults.*

The internalizing, or emotional, component may drive disruptive or maladaptive externalizing behaviors, from task avoidance to physical aggression. Students with EBD may benefit from behavior-specific praise (**BSP**) from teachers to address the internalizing component that will lead to an increase of on-task behavior and work completion (Allday et al., 2012). For example, a teacher might say something like "Steven, I noticed you were angry when I told you to wait to go to the drinking fountain. I am proud of you for staying in your seat and not throwing chairs when you were angry at me; I think you are learning to stay calm." This praise is specific because the teacher told Steven the exact behavior she was praising (staying in his seat and not throwing chairs) instead of using vague praise by saying "Good job, Steven." Vague praise does not allow Steven to know what he did well. Verbal and physical aggression are also common behaviors exhibited by students with EBD (Taylor & Smith, 2019). The social behavioral needs of students with EBD may vary, and as such, each behavior needs to be addressed specifically and explicitly. For example, an intervention that says "be good" is too broad. Instead, a more specific intervention for a student with EBD might be to use the request "May I take a break to regain calm?" when the student is feeling frustrated and needs to pause working on a math problem.

Summary

While students with disabilities vary on the level of support they will need, there is significant overlap in their academic, social-emotional, and behavioral characteristics and needs, as indicated in Table 6.1.

TABLE 6.1 Academic, Social-Emotional, and Behavioral Needs of Students with Disabilities

Disability	Academic Needs	Social-Emotional Needs	Behavioral Needs
Specific Learning Disabilities	Reading, Written Expression, Mathematics, Oral Expression, or Listening Comprehension	Low Self-Esteem, Depression, Anxiety, Poor Interpersonal Skills	Procrastination or Task Initiation, Work or Task Avoidance
Communication Disorders (Speech or Language Impairment)	Expressive and Receptive Language (understanding and expressing language). Sound Production (speech)	Pragmatic Language (nonverbal social aspects of language), Poor Interpersonal Skills	Aggression, Social Withdrawal
Other Health Impairments	Executive Functioning Skill and Attention/Focus (all areas of achievement)	Poor Interpersonal Skills	Hyperactive or Impulsive Behaviors Hyper- or Hypo-focus on Classroom Stimuli
Autism Spectrum Disorder	Reading, Written Expression, Mathematics, Communication	Poor Interpersonal Relationships, Pragmatic Communication	Restricted or Repetitive Patterns of Behavior Interests: Seemingly Meaningless Movement (hand flapping, rocking, hyper- or hypo-arousal

Disability	Academic Needs	Social-Emotional Needs	Behavioral Needs
Developmental Delay	Reading, Written Expression, Mathematics, Communication, Fine or Gross Motor Skills	Social Skills Development in Relation to Age/Grade	Behavioral Skills Developmental in Relation to Age/Grade
Intellectual Disability	Basic Academic Skills, Reading, Written Expression, Mathematics, Oral Expression, Listening Comprehension, Functional Academics	Social Skills Developmental in Relation to Age/Grade: Self-esteem, Gullibility, Social Understanding	Behavioral Skills Developmental in Relation to Age/Grade: Task Initiation and Avoidance, earned Helplessness
Emotional Behavioral Disorder	Reading, Written Expression, Mathematics, Communication	Poor Interpersonal Relationships, Depression or Feelings of Sadness, or Feelings Incongruent with the Situation	Task Avoidance and Verbal or Physical Aggression

Source: National Center for Education Statistics (NCES), 2020. The condition of education—Children and Youth with Disabilities. Indicator, May 2020. Retrieved from https://nces.ed.gov/programs/coe/indicator_cgg.asp

In accordance with the IDEA, it is important that students with disabilities be educated in the least restrictive environment possible. If they are benefiting meaningfully from being in general education with their peers without disabilities, the general education classroom remains the least restrictive environment. What that means is that most students with disabilities spend 80% or more of their school day in general education classrooms. As such, general education teachers are often the teacher of service, or the person responsible for ensuring that students are receiving appropriate support in the general education classroom. In the following chapters (Chapters 7, 8, and 9), we will discuss frameworks for providing interventions and supports, and examples of research-based intervention strategies that can be implemented by general education teachers within the general education classroom to help support students with disabilities to engage in and complete grade level expectations. Although this chapter primarily discussed the needs of students with disabilities, it is important to note that students with disabilities also demonstrate strengths. Student strengths are just as varied and student specific as their needs. When discussing how to work with students with disabilities, it is important to take a strengths-based approach.

Test Your Knowledge

1. Choose two incidence disabilities from Chapter 6 and create a visual (e.g., Venn diagram, table) that presents the similarities and differences between their academic, social-emotional, and behavioral needs.
2. Discuss how the **inclusive education** movement impacts the work of general education teachers with respect to students with disabilities.

Apply Your Knowledge

As part of the IEP team, you are asked to give some recommendations for appropriate accommodations for a student's IEP in your classroom.

Ask

Ask yourself the following question to help guide your reading.

- Which disability category presented in this chapter do you think you will likely need to know more about to prepare for your future students with disabilities in your classroom?

Read

Read the following sections.

- Accommodations and Student Needs
  - See Table 3.1, Sample Accommodations, in Chapter 3 (p. 32)
  - See Table 6.1, Academic, Social Emotional, and Behavioral Needs of Students with Disabilities (p. 74)

Tell

Tell your response.

- Choose one accommodation from Chapter 3, Table 3.1 you think will address an academic need of the same and provide an explanation of how it relates to the student's need.
- Choose one accommodation that will address a social-emotional need and provide an explanation of how it relates to the student's need.
- Choose one accommodation that will address a behavioral need and provide an explanation of how it relates to the student's need.

References

Alesi, M., Rappo, G., & Pepi, A. (2012). Self-esteem at school and self-handicapping in childhood: Comparisons of groups with learning disabilities. *Psychological Reports: Disability & Trauma, 11* (3), 952–962.

Allday, R. A., Hinkson-Lee, K., Hudson, T., Neilsen-Gatti, S., Kleinke, A., & Russel, C. S. (2012). Training general educators to increase behavior specific praise: Effects on students with EBD. *Behavioral Disorders, 37*(2), 87–98.

American Psychological Association (APA). (2013). *Diagnostic and statistical manual of mental disorders* (5th ed.). https://doi.org/10.1176/appi.books.9780890425596

American Speech-Language-Hearing Association. (1993). *Definitions of communication disorders and variations* [Relevant Paper]. Available from www.asha.org/policy.

Doyle, M. B., & Giangreco, M. (2013). Guiding principles for including high school students with intellectual disabilities in general education classes. *American Secondary Education, 42*(1), 57–72.

DuPaul, G., Morgan, P., Farkas, G., Hillemeier, M., & Maczuge, S. (2016). Academic and social functioning associated with attention deficit/hyperactivity disorder: Latent class analyses of trajectories from kindergarten to fifth grade. *Journal of Abnormal Child Psychology, 44*, 1425–1438. doi:10.1007/s10802-016-0126-z

Forness, S. R., Kim, J., & Walker, H. M. (Winter, 2012). Prevalence of students with EBD: Impact on general education. *Beyond Behavior*, 3–10.

Gacek, M., Smolén, T., & Pilecka, W. (2017). Consequences of learned helplessness and recognition in the state of cognitive exhaustion in persons with mild intellectual disabilities. *Advances in Cognitive Psychology, 13*(1), 42–51. doi: 10.5709/acp-0205-6

Garwood, J. D., McKenna, J. W., Roberts, G. J., Ciullo, S., & Shin, M. (2021). Knowledge interventions for students with emotional and behavioral disorders: A meta-analysis. *Behavior Modification, 45*(1), 147–176.

Gregg, K. (2017). Communication disorders and challenging behaviors: Supporting children's functional communication goals in the classroom. *Early Childhood Education Journal, 45*(445–452). doi: 10.1007/s10643-016-0789-7

Greven, C., Asherson, P., Rijsdijk, F., & Plomin, R. (2011). A longitudinal twin study on the association between inattentive and hyperactive-impulsive ADHD symptoms. *Journal of Abnormal Psychology, 39*, 623–632. doi: 10.1007/s10802-011-9513-7

Hallahan, D., Kauffman, J., & Pullen, P. (2019). *Exceptional learners: An introduction to special education* (14th ed.). Pearson.

Individuals with Disability Education Act [IDEA]. (2016). Retrieved from https://www.gpo.gov/fdsys/pkg/FR-2016-12-19/pdf/2016-30190.pdf

Leffert, J. S., Siperstein, G. N., & Widaman, K. F. (February, 2010). Social perception in children with intelectual disabiilties: The interpretation of benign and hostile intention. *Journal of Intellectual Disability Research, 54*(2), 168–180.

MacDonald, R., Parry-Cruwys, D., & Peterson, P. (2018). Behavioral Treatments In E. Hollander, R. J. Hagerman, & D. Fein, *Autism Spectrum Disorders* (195–225). American Psychiatric Association Publishing.

Myers, J., Hill, A. P., Zuckerman, K., & Fombonne, E. (2018). Epidemiology. In E. Hollander, R. J. Hagerman, and D. Fein (Eds.), *Autism spectrum disorders* (pp. 1–48). American Psychiatric Association Publishing.

National Center for Education Statistics (NCES). (2020). The condition of education: Children and youth with disabilities. *Indicator*, May 2020. Retrieved from https://nces.ed.gov/programs/coe/indicator_cgg.asp

National Center of Educational Outcomes (NCEO). (2016). Students with Disabilities. Retrieved from https://nceo.info/student_groups/students_with_disabilities

Oldenhof, H., Jansen, L., Ackermann, K., Baker, R., Batchelor, M., Baumann, S., Bernhard, A., Clanton, R., Dochnal, R., Fehlbaum, L. V., Fernandez-Rivas, A., Goergen, S., Gonzalez de Artaza Lavesa, M., Gonzalez-Madruga, K., Gonzalez-Torres, M. A., Gundlach, M., Lotte van der Hoeven, M., Kalogerakis, Z., Kapornai, K., Kieser, M., … Popma, A. (2020). Psychophysiological responses to sadness in girls and boys with conduct disorder. *Journal of Abnormal Psychology*. Advance online publication. http://dx.doi.org/10.1037/abn000052

Tafla, T. L., Decio Brunoni, D., Carreiro, L. R. R., Seabra, A. G., da Silva, L. A, Bastos, D. C. S., Rossi, A. C., Santos, P. H. A., & Teixeira, M. C. T. V. (2021). Diagnosis: An analytical framework for the identification of elementary school students with intellectual disability. *Frontiers in Education, 6*, 1–12.

Tassé, M., Schalook, R., Balboni, G., Bersani, H., Borthwick-Duffy, S., Spreat, S., Thissen, D., Widaman, K., & Zhang, D. (2012). The construct of adaptive behavior: Its conceptualization, measurement, and use in the field of intellectual disability. *American Journal of Intellectual and Developmental Disabilities, 117*(4), 291–303. https://doi-org.proxyiub.uits.iu.edu/10.1352/1944-7558-117.4.291

Taylor, G. G., & Smith, S. W. (2019). Teacher reports of verbal aggression in school settings among students with emotional and behavioral disorders. *Journal of Emotional and Behavioral Disorders, 27*(1), 52–64.

U.S. Department of Education, Office for Civil Rights (1973). *Free Appropriate Public Education for Students with Disabilities: Requirements Under Section 504 of the Rehabilitation Act of 1973*, Washington, DC, 2010.

Figure Credit

Frameworks for Educating All Learners

This chapter focuses on ways the academic, social-emotional, and behavioral needs of students with disabilities can be supported in the general education classroom. In the first section, we discuss how Universal Design for Learning (UDL) is used as a foundation to engage all students in the learning process. The second part of the chapter discusses Multi-Tiered Systems of Supports (MTSS), specifically three-tiered system of supports, that address academic, behavioral, and social-emotional needs. We will discuss two examples of MTSS: Positive Behavioral Interventions and Supports (PBIS) and Response to Intervention (RTI). Additionally, this chapter provides guidance on how to choose research-based, evidence-informed, or peer-reviewed interventions and strategies to meet the needs of students with disabilities.

In this chapter, readers will:

- Learn the definition of **research-based** practices, which includes instruction, interventions, and strategies;
- Learn about **Universal Design for Learning (UDL)** principles;
- Understand the relationship between **Positive Behavioral Interventions and Supports (PBIS)** and **Response to Intervention (RTI)**, two multitiered systems of support;
- Gain insight on how providing a multimodal approach to learning supports all learners.

All Future Educators
General and special educators often work together to help support all learners, not just those with IEPs.

Elementary General Education
Multi-Tiered Systems of Supports (MTSS) is a framework that is most often used at the elementary school level to identify students for more intensive instruction or interventions.

Secondary General Education
Universal Design for Learning (UDL) is a framework for instruction that engages learners, encourages teachers to present information in more than one way, and allows students to express their understanding in a variety of ways.

Special Education
Knowing how to find research-based interventions is important to the MTSS process. Special educators are often included on schoolwide interventions or MTSS teams in their schools to help develop Interventions and strategies for all learners in need, and not just for those on their caseload (students with IEPs assigned to them).

Undergraduates Interested in Disability Laws
The MTSS process can be used to benefit students with disabilities by providing a framework for early identification and services.

After reading this chapter, readers will:

- Define **research-based** practices;
- Discuss what occurs at each tier of the RTI and PBIS frameworks;
- Describe the how the RTI and PBIS frameworks support all learners;
- Apply the principles of UDL to accommodate for students' needs.

In 2004, the No Child Left Behind (NCLB) Act, the federal law that guides the education of students in general education, included expectations that K–12 educational programming should reflect best practices and provide evidence they adhere to "rigorous scientific research" (U.S. DOE, 2007), otherwise known as research-based programs and practices. **Research-based** programs and practices refers to programs and practices that have undergone systematic, rigorous, and objective research which has resulted in valid and reliable outcomes (U.S. DOE, 2007). The terms *evidence-informed* or *peer-reviewed* are synonymous terms to research-based programs. In the following sections of this chapter, we discuss two research-based frameworks for supporting all learners in general education settings. These are Universal Design for Learning (UDL) and Multi-Tiered Systems of Supports (MTSS).

Universal Design for Learning Principles

Learner variability and diversity exist in every classroom (Courey et al., 2012; Rao & Meo, 2016). The inclusion education reform movement guarantees that general education teachers teach a larger variety of students with a wide variety of learning needs. As such, all teachers will need to develop skills to teach a diverse group of learners (Courey et al., 2012). Students vary in how quickly and through which modes they understand and process information. Students also differ in their abilities to demonstrate knowledge (Rao & Meo, 2016). It is important to remember that variability is not just limited to the skills students have learned and their capacity to learn, but it also comes from their backgrounds and cultures. All teachers can address this variability among their students by providing flexible pathways within the lesson, which proactively support diverse learners (Rao & Meo, 2016). **Universal Design for Learning (UDL)** is a strengths-based framework for teaching all learners. UDL principles intend to provide flexibility in instruction and attempts to make learning materials accessible for all learners. UDL provides opportunities for students with varied levels of achievement and learning challenges who struggle to learn.

> *Variability is not just limited to the skills students have learned and their capacity to learn, but it also comes from their backgrounds and cultures.*

The UDL framework is based on findings in neuroscience, which describes the three main neural networks that are activated in the human brain activities during instruction: (1) recognition, or what students use to understand what they see, hear, or read; (2) strategic, or the way learners organize and express their thoughts and ideas; and (3) affective, or how students became and remain engaged in instruction. The above research-based findings gave way to creating the UDL framework (Al-Azawei et al., 2016). According to Courey et al. (2012), UDL principles revolve around a variety of ways for students to participate in instruction through different modes of *representation* (the what of learning), *action and expression* (the how of learning), and *engagement* (the why of learning).

Principles of UDL

1. **Representation** refers to how instructional materials are designed. This could mean representing instructional materials in written text, through videos, through audio text, and with visual supports, such as diagrams. Additionally, under the representation principle, teachers are encouraged to ask students questions to activate prior knowledge for purposes of helping them make connections between what they already know and new material that they are currently learning. (Courey et al., 2012)

2. **Action or Expression** deals with alternative ways students can communicate and demonstrate their understanding of the instructional materials. Typically, knowledge is assessed through paper-and-pencil tests. However, under the action or expression UDL principle, students can demonstrate their knowledge through a variety of means, such as visual or oral presentations, hands-on projects, or by creating their own story problems. (Courey et al., 2012)

3. **Engagement** is defined as "stimulating students' interest and motivation to learn" (Courey et al., 2012, p. 10). Engaging students in the learning process means finding ways to pique their interest and sustain their attention with the instructional content. Engagement can be achieved through representation, and action and expression. In addition, it can be achieved through teaching students how to monitor their own performance. Most importantly, students can be engaged through the relationships that teachers have with their students. (Courey et al., 2012)

UDL and Academic Standards

Academic standards are used to articulate shared expectations of what students should learn. In the US, the Common Core State Standards (CCSS) are comprised of the learning targets for students K–12 for English language arts and mathematics. The CCSS specifically refer to students with disabilities and the use of UDL to ensure access to the general education curriculum. The standards promote engaging students in instruction through the three principles of UDL. Rao and Meo (2016) suggest that engaging students with disabilities can be achieved by providing appropriate and individualized supports (engagement), including multiple means of presenting information (representation) and allowing students to demonstrate their understanding in a diverse manner (action and expression).

UDL Lesson Plans

Key terms for discussing UDL lesson plans include *multiple sensory modalities, flexible groupings, adjusting instructional pace, and increased efficiency of instruction* (Courey et al., 2012). Multiple sensory modalities refer to the different ways learners can access and express information through more than one sense. Flexible grouping can refer to grouping students together based on similar needs, or by placing students in groups based on their strengths to foster independence. Depending on how quickly students gain understanding of the instruction, the pacing of the instruction can be adjusted to meet the needs of the whole class, for small groups of students, or for individual students. Consistent with the Chapter 5 discussion on collaboration between educators, UDL lesson planning also provides opportunities for co-teaching with special education teachers, who will work alongside general education teachers (Courey et al., 2012) to provide additional support to students in need within the general education setting. All these elements combined can create more efficient instruction, where all students are receiving the support they need and learning at a pace that is appropriate for them.

The UDL principles can be applied to the four components of lesson planning (Courey et al., 2012): lesson goals, materials, methods, and assessment. UDL-inspired lesson planning positively enhances student academic self-image, academic performance, engagement, satisfaction, and self-efficacy. UDL-inspired lesson planning has also been shown to help close the learning gap between students with disabilities and their non-disabled peers (Al-Azawei et al., 2016). UDL lesson plans are proactive plans to meet the needs of all learners, rather than retroactively teach learners after the initial plan has failed to reach them (Courey et al., 2012). Teachers trained in UDL tend to create lesson plans that use at least one novel manner to deliver content, engage students, and assess student learning in ways that were otherwise inaccessible in traditional forms of teaching (Courey et al., 2012). UDL lesson plans provide opportunities for students with various strengths and ranges in abilities, such as seeing, hearing, speaking, reading, writing, and understanding oral language. Student abilities may also include executive functioning skills, like problem solving, planning, prioritizing, organizing, and memory.

> *UDL lesson plans are proactive plans to meet the needs of all learners, rather than retroactively teach learners after the initial plan has failed to reach them.*

Multi-Tiered Systems of Support (MTSS)

In 2004, the NCLB issued guidance to ensure that all students would receive a high-quality education, which includes provisions to support learning in the early years to prevent future learning difficulties and provide information to parents about student progress (U.S. DOE, 2007). High-quality education also includes the implementation of school-based models that provide a framework for earlier identification and intervention for at-risk students that include assessment and data-based progress monitoring (Eagle et al., 2015). The Multi-Tiered System of Support (MTSS) is a conceptual framework based on theoretical, empirical, and practical considerations (Eagle et al., 2015), with the goal of meeting the needs of all learners (Dulaney et al., 2013). MTSS is primarily focused on identifying and intervening in areas of educational need. However, it should be noted that MTSS also strives to identify student strengths to mitigate areas of concern.

The core components of MTSS are data-based decision-making, curricular and instructional methodology, evidence-based or research-based interventions, and systematic problem-solving procedures (Eagle et al., 2015). Data-based decision-making includes universal screeners designed to identify student needs and implementation of research-based interventions. In addition, MTSS also promotes progress monitoring that informs educational decisions (Eagle et al.). What this means is that throughout the intervention process, student progress is monitored frequently to determine if goals have been met, or if additional interventions are necessary. Within MTSS, there are schoolwide problem-solving frameworks that focus on academics, such as **Response to Intervention (RTI)**, and behavior, such as **Positive Behavioral Interventions and Supports (PBIS)**. In the following sections, the authors provide an overview of the main concepts associated with RTI and PBIS. Chapters 8 and 9 will provide a more in-depth discussion of how RTI and PBIS are implemented in school and classroom settings.

RTI and PBIS

RTI and PBIS are examples of multi-tiered systems of support. Both use a three-tiered system of supports. Charlton et al. (2020) describe the three-tier system as follows:

Tier 1 is the foundation and refers to the district-wide, schoolwide, or classroom-wide curriculum for behavior and academics. As such, it is referred to as the universal level of supports that every student in general education receives. At the Tier 1 level, it is expected that approximately 80% of students will be successful without additional supports or interventions.

Tier 2 refers to targeted small-group interventions that focus on a particular skill or sets of skills. Students receiving Tier 2 interventions are grouped together by similar need. Approximately 15% to 20% of students are successful with the additional support provided at this tier.

Tier 3 refers to the interventions and supports that are provided to students who have demonstrated a need for more intensive and individualized interventions beyond levels 1 and 2. Approximately 5% of students receive Tier 3 supports. Students who do not find success at the Tier 3 level may be referred for educational evaluation.

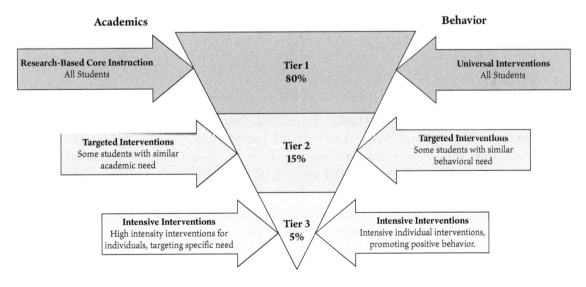

FIGURE 7.1 Academic and behavioral (RTI and PBIS) hierarchy of supports

Providing academic and behavioral supports to students using the RTI and PBIS is not without its challenges. The primary challenge is that the effectiveness of interventions and strategies depends on the fidelity of implementation (Charlton et al., 2020). This means that the interventions and strategies must be implemented as written in the research- and evidenced-based resources. Charlton et al. found seven critical factors that can hinder the fidelity of implementation of RTI and PBIS:

1. competing priorities, philosophies, and practices;
2. ineffective professional development models;
3. hiring, retention, and turnover;
4. varying levels of readiness of districts to implement;
5. limited or restricted funding;
6. inadequate data systems; and
7. inadequate support from state leaders.

> *The primary challenge is that the effectiveness of interventions and strategies depends on the fidelity of implementation.*

For schools and districts to be successful in implementing MTSS like RTI and PBIS, district and state leaders, including building-level administrators, must provide appropriate supports to schools. Support can look like providing adequate resources, which can include funding, personnel, and training. Support can also refer to choosing practices that align with MTSS philosophies and practices, as well as using language that is consistent with MTSS philosophies and practices. Additionally, changing the district mindset to align with MTSS philosophies and practices can shift district, teacher, parent, and even student priorities away from letter and percentage grades to focus on growth. Finally, it is important to remember when discussing MTSS, RTI, and PBIS that the tiers refer to the supports and expectations at each level, and not the students who are receiving the tiered supports. In other words, teachers and other adults within the school are responsible for providing Tier 1, 2, and 3 supports and should not refer to students as Tier 1, Tier 2, or Tier 3 students.

Summary

In this chapter, we defined the different ways research-based practices, including interventions and strategies, are used to support all learners. NCLB provides guidance to include research-based practices designed to improve educational outcomes for all learners. Quality, research-based Tier 1 instruction applies all the principles of UDL to reach all learners in general education classrooms; however, UDL principles are also used at Tiers 2 and 3 to provide additional supports to the general education curriculum. Remember that all interventions and strategies are in addition to general education curriculum and are not meant to supplement or replace general education curriculum and instruction.

Test Your Knowledge

1. Define **research-based** practices.
2. What are the three main principles of **UDL**?
3. What are the core components of **MTSS**?

Apply Your Knowledge

Research-Based Practices for Instruction

It is important for educators to understand the importance of selecting research-based intervention for instruction.

Ask

Ask yourself the following question to help guide your reading.

- What researched-based interventions can I implement in my future classroom?

Read

Read the following:

- See Table 6.1, Academic, Social-Emotional, and Behavioral Needs of Students with Disabilities (p. 74)
- Teaching All Learners (p. 80)
- **P**lanning **R**ealistic **I**mplementation and **M**aintenance by **E**ducators (PRIME, 2014) steps for selecting research-based interventions:

1. Identify the issue of concern and collect baseline data. Baseline data is the student's current level of functioning in the academic, social-emotional, or behavioral areas of concern.
2. Search the internet, books, and primary sources for interventions.
3. Consider the benefits and disadvantages of implementing the intervention in the general education classroom. Is the intervention available to use, affordable to use, and feasible within the scope of practices and resources within the school?
4. Select an appropriate research-based or evidence-based intervention.

Tell

Tell your response.

Review the steps for PRIME (2014) in the **READ** section and answer the following prompts.

1. From Table 6.1, choose an academic, social-emotional, or behavioral concern.
2. Choose a research-based intervention. You may use online databases, books, or other primary sources.
3. Describe the possible benefits and disadvantages of implementing the intervention in your future classroom.

References

Al-Azawei, A., Sereneli, F., & Lundqvist, K. (2016). Universal design for learning (UDL): A content analysis of peer reviewed journal papers from 2012 to 2015. *Journal of the Scholarship of Teaching and Learning, 16*(3), 39–56. doi: 10.14434/josotl.v16i3.19295

Charlton, C., Sabey, C., Young, E., & Moulton, S. (2020). Interpreting critical incidents in implementing multi-tiered system of supports through an active implementation framework. *Exceptionality, 28*(3), 161–175. https://doi.org/10.1080/09362835.2020.1727332

Courey, J., Tappe, P., Siker, J., & LePage, P. (2012). Improved lesson planning with universal design for learning (UDL). *Teacher Education and Special Education, 36*(1), 7–27, doi: 10.1177/0888406412446178

Dulaney, S., Hallman, P., & Wall, G. (2013). Superintendent perceptions of multi-tiered systems of supports (MTSS): Obstacles and opportunities for school system reform. *AASA Journal of Scholarship and Practice, 10*(2), 30–45.

Eagle, J., Dowd-Eagle, S., Snyder, A., & Gibbons Holtzman, E. (2015). Implementing a multi-tiered system of support (MTSS: Collaboration between school psychologist and administrators to promote systems-level change). *Journal of Educational and Psychological Consultations, 25*, 160–177. doi: 10.1080/10474412.2014.929960

Planning Realistic Implementation and Maintenance by Educators (PRIME). (2014). How to select evidence-based intervention: A guide. Retrieved 09/12/2021 from https://implementationscience.uconn.edu/wpcontent/uploads/sites/1115/2014/12/PRIME_quickguide_edvidence-based_intervention.pdf

Rao, K., & Meo, G. (2016). Using universal design for learning to design standards-based lessons. *Special Issue–Student Diversity*, 1–12. doi: 10.1177/2158244016680688

U.S. Department of Education (U.S. DOE). (2007). No child left behind: Help for students and their families. https://www2.ed.gov/parents/academic/involve/2006toolkit/nclb-en.html

Behavioral Interventions to Improve Learning

When students behave in a way which disrupts the general education classroom, it not only interferes with the education of the misbehaving student, but also interferes with the learning experience of all other students in the classroom (Little & Akin-Little, 2017). Many general education teachers respond to disruptive classroom behaviors from students by removing them from the classroom (Leggio & Terras, 2019). However, removing students who disrupt classroom learning does not, in and of itself, teach students how to behave in an appropriate manner. Research has shown that students who are removed from the general education classroom in response to disruptive classroom behavior experience loss of instructional time and increased risk for contact with the juvenile justice system (Martinez et al., 2016). Therefore, removing students for classroom misbehavior is educationally counterproductive and creates a social wedge between misbehaving students and the rest of the individuals in the general education classroom.

General education teachers may not intentionally set out to cause educational harm to students who engage in disruptive behavior. Likely, general education teachers remove students because they have behavior and classroom management skills deficits. As such, removing a student who disrupts instruction is an immediate, albeit temporary, solution. General education teachers need better classroom management skills to establish and maintain order

All Future Educators
All student behavior is the result of an internalized process. The thoughts, feelings, and beliefs a student holds, as well as health conditions, impact the way the student's brain processes and reacts to information.

Elementary General Education
Positive reinforcements or rewards for appropriate student behavior helps students to develop the skills they need to succeed academically, behaviorally, and socially.

Secondary General Education
Intentional modeling of appropriate responses to conflict will help students learn how to respond appropriately in difficult situations.

Special Education Educators
Student misbehavior may result in learning deficits due to missed instructional time. However, students with learning difficulties may also engage in misbehavior to avoid undesirable academic tasks.

Undergraduates Interested in Disability Laws
Removing students with disabilities from instruction when the behavior is a manifestation of the disability may violate their rights under the IDEA, Section 504, and the ADA.

among all students and skills to promote prosocial behavior in students who exhibit disruptive classroom behavior.

In this chapter, readers will:

- Review the characteristics of students with disabilities who exhibit behavioral challenges;
- Consider the reasons students with disabilities engage in disruptive behavior;
- Understand the importance for general education teachers to develop skills to respond effectively to students who display disruptive behavior.

After reading this chapter, readers will be able to:

- Discuss the different levels of behavioral support associated with the PBIS framework.
- Identify different strategies to use at each level of the PBIS framework to assist students with behavioral challenges.
- Know which strategies can provide behavioral support to a variety of students in the general education classroom.
- Know the benefits of collaborating with special education teachers when students need help in managing their behavior in the general education classroom beyond that which the general education teacher provides.

Students with Disabilities and Disruptive Behavior

Chapter 6 provides a list of the disabilities recognized under the IDEA along with the academic, social-emotional, and behavioral needs of the categories considered high-incidence disabilities. In this chapter, we highlight the behavioral characteristics of students with specific learning disabilities (SLD), attention deficit hyperactivity disorder (ADHD), and emotional and behavioral disorders (EBD) as examples of how students with different disabilities demonstrate similar characteristics. As discussed in previous chapters, although the IDEA uses the term *emotional disturbance* (ED), many scholars use the term in emotional and behavioral disorders (EBD) because it reflects both the internalizing and externalizing behaviors common among this population. While ADHD is not a disorder recognized as its own category, students with ADHD who are served under the IDEA do so under the other health impairment (OHI) category. Students with SLD, ADHD, and EBD often experience academic underachievement and behavioral problems (Nelson et al., 2011).

It is not likely that general education teachers indiscriminately remove students with disabilities without reason. As indicated previously in Chapter 1, general education teachers are responding to disruptive classroom behaviors which violate expected classroom rules when they remove a student from the classroom. For example, a student with ADHD in the fourth grade may repeatedly disrupt instruction by getting up from their seat during a time when the teacher is giving directions on an assignment. Another example might be an eighth-grade student with SLD who rips up a test instead of submitting it for grading. Yet another example might be a tenth-grade student who walks out of the classroom while a general education teacher is confronting the student for using profanity in the middle of an argument with a peer. In each of these examples, the teacher may send the students with disabilities who did not adhere to classroom expectations to the school principal's office. Table 8.1 provides a list of some of the overlapping behavioral challenges exhibited by students with SLD, ADHD, and EBD.

TABLE 8.1 Overlapping Characteristics of SLD, ADHD, and EBD

Students with SLD	Students with ADHD	Students with EBD
• Academic underachievement • Executive function deficits • Communication and language deficits • High frustration levels • Interpersonal difficulties	• Academic underachievement • Executive function deficits • Concentration problems • Interpersonal difficulties	• Academic underachievement • Executive function deficits • Interpersonal difficulties • Communication and language problems

Why Do Students with Disabilities Engage in Disruptive Classroom Behavior?

There are different reasons to explain why students with disabilities engage in disruptive behavior. Nelson et al. (2011) describe three models. One model states that academic difficulties cause students to develop behavioral problems. In this explanation of the relationship between academics and behavior, students act out to avoid academic tasks they cannot perform. In other words, students with academic disabilities mask their disabilities by misbehaving. For many students, misbehaving during instruction ensures them that the teacher will refer them out of the class for disruption. Thus, the student avoids the embarrassment of not being able to perform academically. A second model suggests that behavioral problems, such as lack of attention, cause academic problems. In this explanation, students are unable to do academic work because they are unable to pay attention to instruction. For example, students with ADHD can do the academic work but they are unable to focus long enough to accomplish the work. A third model suggests a reciprocal relationship in which the two impact each other and indicates successful interventions in behavior will likely lead to improved academic outcomes and vice versa.

Yet another reason some students with disabilities misbehave is because many general education teachers lack preparation to meet the behavioral or social skill needs common among students with disabilities. Teacher preparation programs typically provide content-specific preparation to their general education candidates (Da Fonte & Barton-Arwood, 2017). Most commonly, special education teachers are the professionals prepared, through their teacher preparation coursework, to know the learning and behavioral characteristics of students with disabilities. Nonpunitive behavioral interventions can help general education teachers develop competencies to manage student behavior and set up their classrooms to increase the likelihood of safeguarding instructional time against behavioral disruptions from students.

Differentiated Behavioral Support for Students in General Education Classrooms

Positive Behavioral Interventions and Supports (PBIS) describes a method of progressive assistance in which teachers offer differentiated support to students based on their behavioral needs. PBIS aims to promote learning for all students by preventing the emergence of misbehavior. PBIS also aims to reduce the number of students who engage in maladaptive behavior by being responsive to all behavior and by meeting students at their behavioral levels (Yong & Cheney, 2013). General educators working under the traditional model of addressing behavior may make faulty assumptions about students and learning. First, general education teachers assume that all students know what behaviors are expected of them. In other words, general education teachers assume that all students know the basic rules of classroom behavior. Another assumption often made by general education teachers is that all students have the skills to follow the classroom rules. In fact, some students know what they ought to do but cannot independently meet behavioral expectations. Finally, general education teachers assume that students are intrinsically motivated to follow behavioral expectations. As such, general education teachers neglect to acknowledge, or reinforce, prosocial behavior in students. That is, teachers often ignore students when they are following the rules. In fact, many general education teachers attend only to behaviors when they are disruptive. This last assumption allows good behavior to go unrewarded, while bad behavior elicits teacher attention.

> *Teachers often ignore students when they are following the rules.*

PBIS is an intentional shift away from the traditional approach to disruptive behavior in which the general education teacher waits to respond punitively when disruptive behavior is observed in a student (Leach & Helf, 2016). PBIS is nonpunitive. Instead, PBIS proactively seeks to teach desirable behavior to all students and provides the necessary support to students who need it to be able to meet behavioral expectations (Wehby & Lane, 2019). PBIS is a three-tiered framework in which educators commit to helping all students develop the behavioral skills that match the school's or the general education teacher's classroom expectations. PBIS is not a packaged program guaranteed to reduce disruptive behavior. Nor is PBIS a silver bullet that makes disruptive behavior disappear simply because the teacher wishes it. In addition, PBIS is not a one-shot vaccine that, once given, automatically immunizes students against misbehavior. Finally, PBIS is not new; it is a derivative of operant conditioning and applied behavior analysis, a system of analyzing the function of disruptive behavior. It has been in use in the field of psychology since the 1960s (Wehby & Lane, 2019). Over the years, a robust body of research evidence has developed, showing the effectiveness of PBIS for changing behaviors on both classroom and schoolwide levels (Ochoa & Rogers-Adkinson, 2012). In the following sections, we provide a description of the PBIS framework with example strategies to use in each tier.

Tier 1 of the PBIS framework focuses on preventing the onset of behavioral problems (Yong & Cheney, 2013). Prevention of behavioral problems is achieved by making behavioral expectations explicit and clear to all students. Under the PBIS framework, rules are clearly explained to all students, and students are given the opportunity to practice expected behaviors. Importantly, those behaviors are rewarded appropriately when they occur (Ochoa & Rogers-Adkinson, 2012; Wehby & Lane, 2019). Acknowledging and rewarding students for appropriate classroom behavior is a critical component of any Tier 1 classroom management program. Table 8.2 shows examples of rewards to reinforce students on a daily and weekly basis and at the end of the semester for meeting classroom behavioral expectations. Figures 8.1 and 8.2 provide two examples created by general education teachers. Of note, both lists explicitly tell the students what the teachers want them to do instead of what the teacher does *not* want them to do. Note the lists are reflective of a language classroom and an art classroom. Importantly, classroom expectations for Tier 1 interventions need to reflect the personality of each teacher and address the classroom expectations of particular settings.

TABLE 8.2 Reinforcement System for a Tier 1 Intervention by Preservice Art Education Candidate

Small Daily Prizes Options	Pen; 1 bonus point; soda; snack; sit by a friend
Medium Weekly Prizes Options	Computer pass; 5 bonus points; homework skip; sit with group of friends
Large Semester Prizes Options	Drop lowest score; 10 bonus points; favorite lunch

FIGURE 8.1 Tier 1 behavior expectations created by future general education Art Education teacher.

FIGURE 8.2 Tier 1 behavior expectations created by future English Education teacher.

Pre-correction and *Choices* are two examples of Tier 1 strategies that general education teachers can use to prevent the development of behavioral problems. *Pre-correction* is a strategy in which general education teachers anticipate the challenges that their students are going to confront. In this strategy, knowledge about student characteristics is important and allows the general education teacher to plan for the needs of students ahead of time. For example, an elementary-level general education teacher who is teaching a third-grade classroom might address students having aversive feelings about working with a different sex group than the one they identify with. The teacher could say something such as, "I know that some of the boys in class might prefer to only work with other boys, and girls in class might prefer to work only with other girls. However, for this activity, I want you to work with someone of a different sex." In the example, teachers anticipated the discomfort among students to work with someone of a different sex and pre-corrected the problem by talking explicitly about their possible hesitation during the educational activity. The important thing to remember about pre-correction is that the teacher anticipates the difficulty some students might have and corrects the problem before it happens.

In providing *choices*, teachers offer students a menu of activities to do. Instructional choices as a strategy are useful because they give students an opportunity to exercise choice-making and they feel like they have self-agency. Students who experience challenges with authority figures might benefit from making choices by being able to put off doing something they dislike or having an option to feel like they are the ones imposing an undesired task upon themselves. The important thing to remember when using instructional choice as a strategy is that once the student makes the choice, the teacher must honor the choice the student made. For example, students who resist doing what general education teachers tell them to do during a reading comprehension assignment might refrain from defying the teacher if there are choices like "You may choose to write out your answer, type your answer, draw a picture of your answer, or record your answer." Research using instructional choice found that students' engagement on tasks increased and behavioral problems decreased (Wehby & Lane, 2019) and aligns with the UDL principle of Action and Expression.

> *The important thing to remember when using instructional choice as a strategy is that once the student makes the choice, the teacher must honor the choice the student made.*

Tier 2 interventions in the PBIS framework focus on providing support to small groups of students with similar needs who require support beyond the first tier to meet behavioral expectations (MacLeod et al., 2016). Tier 2 interventions are also called targeted interventions because they focus on providing behavioral support to a subgroup of students at risk for developing a particular disorder (Farmer et al., 2021). Research suggests that 10% to 15% of students in any classroom will need additional support to meet the general education teacher's classroom expectations for behavior. Therefore, based on this research, a classroom of 30 students will have at least a handful of students who will need additional support from the general education teacher to be able to meet classroom expectations. As with primary interventions, Tier 2 interventions must be clear and positive. Leach and Helf (2016) indicate that it is important for general education teachers to remember that Tier 2 interventions are to help redirect students to allow them to find success in the classroom. Therefore, when general education teachers intervene with students who need additional behavioral support, the goal must be to get those students refocused on learning. Small groups refer to students who demonstrate a similar behavioral need, like students who are late to school or absent from school or students who struggle to submit completed work.

> *When general education teachers intervene with students who need additional behavioral support, the goal must be to get those students refocused on learning.*

The *Check-in/Check-out* (CICO) intervention is one of the most effective evidence-based Tier 2 interventions in the PBIS framework (MacLeod et al., 2016). Behavior Education Program (BEP) is another name for the CICO intervention. As the name suggests, students using this intervention check in at the start of the day with a CICO coordinator. At the elementary school level, the CICO coordinator might be a nurse, or a paraprofessional. At the middle school or high school levels, the CICO coordinator could be a coach or a paraprofessional. The important thing about the CICO coordinators is that they would be responsible to make sure the students receiving Tier 2 behavioral support are ready to begin the day with all required materials related to their behavior education program. An example of a Tier 2 intervention is a small group of students who have difficulties arriving to second period ready to submit homework assignments. Table 8.3 is a checklist that the CICO coordinator can use. The checklist can serve to help students to make sure that they each have completed the homework assignment and that it is readily available for submission at the start of the second period. During the check-in, the CICO coordinator might also remind students why it is important to submit homework and would provide words of encouragement to the student as a way of motivating them to carry out the behavioral expectation. At the end of the day, or at another designated part of the day, the student would check out with the same CICO coordinator to review the behavioral accomplishments of the day. Table 8.3 is an example of a CICO checklist and Daily Progress Report (DPR) to keep the student informed on his or her progress on homework completion.

TABLE 8.3 Tier 2 Homework Completion Checklist

Steps to Check Today Date: Week's goal: Submit my homework, even if it is incomplete.		
	Yes ✓	No ✓
1. Locate my homework due at start of second period.		
2. Is my name at the top of the homework assignment?		
3. Is my homework complete?		
4. Place assignment in folder that says "Homework Due"		

Suggested points of discussion at check-in between student and CICO coordinator:

1. How do you feel about your readiness to submit homework today?
2. What might you do differently tonight or tomorrow morning to improve your work toward the goal of homework completion and submission?

Note from CICO coordinator to student:

> [I am proud of you today because ...]

Note to self from student:

> [I am proud of myself today because ...]

Daily Progress Reports (DPRs) are important in CICO interventions because they provide visual reminders of behavioral expectations and are a permanent record of the students' progress. Research on the use of CICO interventions show that elementary and middle school level students benefited from daily reminders of behavioral expectations as indicated by increased engagement in school activities and a reduction of behavioral problems (MacLeod et al., 2016).

Tier 3 interventions (or tertiary interventions) focus on providing individual support to students who, despite having access to the previous two levels of behavioral supports, continue to be unable to meet behavioral expectations (Yong & Cheney, 2013). Under the PBIS framework, it is typical for about 1% to 5% of any student population to need individual behavioral support (MacLeod et al., 2016). Tier 3 behavioral supports represent the most intense behavior program reserved for students with the highest levels of behavioral needs (Wehby & Lane, 2019). Tier 3 interventions use applied behavior analysis (ABA), a technique used in psychology to study (or analyze) the function a behavior serves (Ochoa & Rogers-Adkinson, 2012). ABA assumes that understanding the function of a behavior will lead to an improved understanding of why a student engages in the behavior, which in turn will allow the interventionist to design a specific behavior intervention program. The ABA that informs Tier 3 interventions is not to be confused with ABA therapy.

The functional behavioral assessment (FBA) is useful because it provides information about why a particular student engages in disruptive behavior (MacLeod et al., 2016). The first step in conducting an FBA is to determine the antecedents to a behavior (what happens immediately before the behavior; define the behavior of concern; and determine what consequences follow when a student engages in misbehavior (what happens after the behavior that may reinforce the behavior). Once the antecedents and consequences are determined, the individuals completing the FBA will propose a hypothesis on the function of the behavior. For example, a student in second grade persistently fights with a peer who sits next to him. After observing the student over a period of time to establish a baseline of the child's behavior, and to observe when and how often the behavior of concern is exhibited, the person conducting the FBA establishes (or notices) that fighting occurs during reading instruction. The observer also notices that when the student fights with another student, the general education teacher issues an office disciplinary referral and removes the student from the classroom. An FBA hypothesis posed by the person conducting the observation might be that the student engages in fighting behavior with another student to be removed from the classroom, which results in the student avoiding having to read.

As previously stated, PBIS and the different levels of interventions associated with the framework are not a magic potion that automatically eradicate disruptive classroom behavior. PBIS is a commitment by a general education teacher to put more effort into teaching students who disrupt instruction-appropriate behaviors, instead of removing them from the opportunity to learn from him or her in the general education classroom. Essentially, general education teachers are not only teaching specific subject matter but are also teaching appropriate social skills and learning skills and behaviors. The Center for PBIS (https://www.pbis.org/pbis/getting-started) provides useful information.

Consequences for Inappropriate Classroom Behavior Under the PBIS Framework

One point to make clear about the PBIS framework is how general education teachers apply consequences when students do not meet behavioral expectations. Nothing in the PBIS framework should be interpreted to suggest that general education teachers cannot respond to students when they do not meet their behavioral expectations. In fact, quite to the contrary, the PBIS encourages general education teachers to respond frequently and as quickly as possible when any student violates the classroom's code of conduct. In other words, all students in a classroom should be expected to contribute to the climate of a classroom in a positive manner. The focus is on recognizing and praising positive behaviors and responding in a nonpunitive way to disruptive behaviors. How general education teachers respond to the breach of classroom code of conduct is what makes PBIS unique and different from the traditional approach to classroom comportment. Punishment has no place in the PBIS framework because punishment is counterproductive (Ochoa et al., 2013). More importantly, punishment does not provide students with opportunities to learn or practice prosocial behavior. General education teachers who adopt the PBIS framework commit themselves to helping students who cannot meet behavioral expectations develop the skills, with consistent and nonpunitive assistance (Leach & Helf, 2016).

The PBIS framework offers a hierarchy of supportive consequences that general education teachers can use to help students who engage in disruptive behavior (Leach & Helf, 2016). First, general education teachers should ignore the behavior from the student who is disruptive in class. Instead, general education teachers should provide overt verbal reinforcement (acknowledgment) to a student in the classroom who is engaged in the alternative and prosocial behavior. For example, if a student is looking over someone's assignment to copy, the teacher could say something like, "I am walking around to monitor that everyone is complying with the classroom expectation of working independently. I see several of you looking at your own papers, thank you. Thank you, Sam, for looking straight at your paper in the assignment. You are doing exactly what I expect you to do." In this way, the student who is looking over at someone else's assignment is aware that the general education teacher is monitoring. More importantly, if the student was not looking over to copy, the general education teacher has not shamed the student. In addition, the teacher also told the students what behavior is expected.

The PBIS hierarchy of supportive consequences also provides reminders, nonverbal and verbal. If a student is distracted or is delaying the start of an assignment, the general education teacher can walk around and give someone a thumbs-up as he holds the book up to read as a nonverbal reminder for the distracted student to begin reading. If the student does not get the hint, then the general education teacher can get closer to the student who is distracted and say something such as, "You have five more minutes to read. I'll wait here for you to start in case you need my help." The PBIS hierarchy of consequences also assumes that if the student does not comply with behavioral expectations, it means that he or she needs help. Therefore, the next thing to do when a student does not engage in the expected behavior is to help them. In this case, the teacher can follow up by saying, "Here, let's read together, I'll read one paragraph, you read the next sentence." Finally, it is important for general education teachers to give students who are frustrated or cannot work an opportunity to decompress. Insisting that a student do something when they are not emotionally ready to engage can heighten frustration. Sometimes, the best thing to do is give students who are not complying an opportunity to gather themselves. Therefore, having a designated place, even for older students, to calm down or relax is also part of the PBIS framework's hierarchy of consequences for behavior.

Benefits of Collaborating with Special Education Teachers in PBIS

There are significant benefits for general education teachers who collaborate with special education teachers. Special education teaching problems typically provide more training than general education teaching programs in thinking about how the arrangement of learning environments impacts a variety of learners. As such, general education teachers stand to benefit from the knowledge that special education teachers have. At the Tier 1 level, general education teachers and special education teachers can work together to make sure classroom expectations are stated in positive language that communicates what behavior is expected of students instead of resorting to the traditional approach common in many general education classrooms, where the rules only tell students what not to do but seldom tell students what behavior they can engage in. General education teachers can structure their classrooms to prevent students from engaging in disruptive behavior by working with the special education teacher to set up classroom expectation (see Figures 8.1 and 8.2).

At the Tier 2 level of the PBIS approach, general education teachers can also benefit from collaborating with a special education teacher. Because special education teachers have, as part of their teacher preparation program, developed skills and strategies to monitor behavior, they can lead the efforts to design small-group behavioral interventions and reinforcement programs that the CICO coordinator can do. In some cases, the special education teacher might also serve as the CICO coordinator if a paraprofessional cannot be used. Additionally, special education teachers can work with general education teachers to train and support the Tier 2 CICO coordinator to implement and monitor Tier 2 interventions. Finally, and of most importance to general education teachers, collaborating with a special education teacher is beneficial because special education teachers may have the training to conduct FBAs. General education teachers should not expect to be able to develop the skills to conduct FBAs after only one class in special education as part of their teacher education programming. However, the way many teacher preparation programs are organized in the present, special education teachers are the ones most likely to have the preparation to conduct Tier 3 interventions or FBAs for students (Da Fonte & Barton-Arwood, 2017).

Summary

General education teachers are justified in their efforts to prevent or minimize the occurrence of disruptive behavior in their classrooms. In fact, their primary professional responsibility is to create positive learning environments where all students can learn. There is substantial research evidence showing that the PBIS framework is more effective than office disciplinary referrals at reducing disruptive behavior and increasing student engagement. The reason PBIS is more effective than punishment (i.e., sending the student to the school principal as a disciplinary measure for disruptive behavior in the classroom) is because general education teachers focus on teaching students how to behave. However unprepared general education teachers might feel to implement PBIS in their classrooms, collaborating with a special education teacher is beneficial for implementing positive behavioral interventions that increase the likelihood more students will be engaged in their academic learning.

Test Your Knowledge

1. What are the most common reasons students engage in disruptive classroom behavior?
2. How is the PBIS framework different from the traditional approach to disruptive classroom behavior?
3. What is involved in each tier of the PBIS framework?
4. How do general education teachers stand to benefit from collaborating with special education teachers in response to students whose behavior disrupts instruction?

Apply Your Knowledge

Use the blank lesson plan provided and refer to Figure 2.2, *Academic, social-emotional, and behavioral needs of students with disabilities* in Chapter 2.

1. Choose a behavioral characteristic.
2. Determine if you will be targeting an individual student (Tier 2) or a small group of students with similar needs (Tier 3).
   a. For a small group of students, discuss the different areas of disability that may be associated with the characteristic you have chosen.
   b. For an individual student, choose an area of disability you are most interested in targeting.
3. Then choose an intervention or strategy that would likely address the characteristics you have chosen. Provide the research-based, evidence-based, or peer-reviewed reference(s).
4. Apply the concepts of **UDL** to a lesson plan to accommodate for students' needs.
   a. For materials, provide at least two examples that would be used for representation, action and expression, and engagement.

b. In the modifications and adaptations section, provide at least one example of how you would change your materials to address representation, action and expression, and engagement specifically to meet the academic need identified in #2.

Universal Design for Learning Lesson Plan Outline

Lesson Plan Topic and Grade Level:

Developed By:

Target Student(s):

IEP Goal
IEP Annual Goal for Students with Disabilities Student name(s): _____ IEP Goals: At the end of _____, the student will be able to _____ with _____ accuracy.

Lesson Objectives
Central Focus Student(s) will understand:

Academic Standard

Materials		
Representation	**Action and Expression**	**Engagement**

Article References

Methods

Lesson Format

Introduction

Procedures	Teacher will...	Student will...
Attending Cue (to gain student attention)		
Anticipatory Set (Preassessment, review, or new information?)		

Body

Procedures	Teacher will...	Student will...
Input (methods and techniques, link to prior learning):		
Modeling (demonstration, video, verbal explanation):		
Guided Practice (prompts, corrective feedback):		
Independent Practice (students demonstrate skill):		

Closure

Assessment			
Students	Exceed Expectations	Meet Expectations	Approaching Expectations
Students will ...			

Modifications and Adaptions		
Representation	Action and Expression	Engagement

(Adapted from Courey et al., 2012)

References

Center for PBIS. (n.d.). Getting started: What is PBIS? Retrieved 09/19/2021 from https://www.pbis.org/pbis/getting-started

Da Fonte, M. A., & Barton-Arwood, S. M. (2017). Collaboration of general and special education teachers: Perspectives and strategies. *Intervention in School and Clinic, 53*(2) 99–106.

Farmer, T. W, Bierman, K. L, Hall, C. M., Brooks, D. S., & Lee, D. L. (2021). Tiered systems of adaptive supports and the individualization of intervention: Merging developmental cascades and correlated constraints perspectives. *Journal of Emotional and Behavioral Disorders, 29*(1) 3–13.

Leach, D., & Helf, S. (2016). Using a hierarchy of supportive consequences to address problem behaviors in the classroom. *Intervention in School and Clinic, 52,* 29–33.

Leggio, J. C., & Terras, K. L. (2019). An investigation of the qualities, knowledge, and skills of effective teachers for students with emotional/behavioral disorders: The teacher perspective. *The Journal of Special Education Apprenticeship, 8*(1), 1–15.

Little, S. G., & Akin-Little, A. (2019). *Behavioral interventions in schools: Evidence-based positive strategies* (2nd ed.). American Psychological Association.

MacLeod, K. S., Hawken, L. S., O'Neil, R. E., & Bundock, K. (2016). Combining tier 2 and tier 3 supports for students with disabilities in general education settings. *Journal of Educational Issue, 2*(2), 331–351.

Martinez, A., McMahon, S., & Treger, S. (2016). Individual- and school-level predictors of student office disciplinary referrals. *Journal of Emotional and Behavioral Disorders, 24*(1)m 30–41.

Nelson, J. R., Lane, K. L., Benner, G. J., & Kim, O. (2011). A best evidence synthesis of literacy instruction on the social adjustment of students with or at-risk for behavior disorders. *Education and Treatment of Children, 34*(1), 141–16.2.

Ochoa, T. A., Otero, T. L., Levy, L. J., & Deskalo, A. Y. (2013). Integration of the school resource officer as liaison between law enforcement and school administration in the discipline of students. *Law Enforcement Executive Forum, 13*(2), 129–136.

Ochoa, T. A., & Rogers-Adkinson, D. (2012). Are positive behavioral interventions and supports effective at reducing misbehavior in students with behavior disorders? In S. Eckes and C. J. Russo (Eds.), *Encyclopedia of education law* (pp. 231–245). Sage Publications.

Wehby, J. H., & Lane, K. L. (2019). Classroom management. In S. G. Little & A. Akin-Little (Eds.), *Behavioral interventions in schools: Evidence-based positive strategies* (pp. 61–76). American Psychological Association. https://doi.org/10.1037/0000126-004

Yong, M. and Cheney, D.A. (2013), Essential features of tier 2 social-behavioral intervention. *Psychology in School, 50* (8), 844–861. https://doi.org/10.1002/pits.21710

Academic Interventions

This chapter focuses on academic interventions for use in the general education setting to facilitate academic growth in students with disabilities. Response to Intervention (RTI) and Universal Design for Learning (UDL) principles are used to engage students, provide them with multisensory and multimodal representations of information, and offer them multiple means of demonstrating their understanding of academic content. Chapter 9 also discusses how support is provided to students, highlighting the different roles of general education teachers, special educators, and other service providers such as speech and language pathologists or occupational therapists. The purpose of this chapter is to help educators learn how to target specific areas of academic need for students.

In this chapter, readers will:

- Learn how RTI is used to inform students' academic needs;
- Develop an understanding of their role in providing academic supports for students with disabilities;
- Gain insight on the different resources available to help develop and implement academic interventions.

All Future Educators
Academic interventions can be implemented at elementary and secondary school levels. When designing materials, keep in mind the students' developmental levels, as well as the skills being addressed.

Elementary General Education
At the elementary school level, teachers typically teach most, if not all, general education content. As such, they will teach, assess, and support student learning in reading, writing, and mathematics.

Secondary General Education
Although secondary teachers typically teach only one content area, they are responsible for more students than their elementary school counterparts. As such, they will collaborate with both special education teachers and general education teachers from other content areas to support student learning across content areas.

Special Education
Although special education teachers have smaller caseloads, all their students have IEPs and require specially designed instruction. Additionally, special education teachers provide support across all school subjects.

Undergraduates Interested in Disability Laws
Interventions should align with students' specific academic needs and IEP goals.

After reading this chapter, readers will:

- Identify academic strategies for use in general education classrooms;
- Demonstrate skills in selecting an appropriate academic strategy to match the characteristics and needs of a student with a disability.

Response to Intervention (RTI)

As indicated in Chapter 7, Response to Intervention (RTI) is the three-tiered system that provides progressive academic support to students in general education classrooms. These supports are *in addition to* the general education curriculum, and they begin at the first tier with evidence-based general education instruction designed for all students. The RTI framework has most often been applied in the elementary school level. In addition, instruction often focuses on basic skill acquisition of elementary level students. However, RTI can also be used at the secondary level to support student academic needs. Implementation of RTI requires parent involvement, which includes providing parents with information about the interventions in use, the learning goals for the student as well as progress the student makes toward those learning goals.

Tier 1 interventions are the building blocks of all learning. At this first tier, all students are periodically screened using a valid screener like a curriculum-based measurement, which provides a baseline for academic skills. The purpose of using the screening tool is to help identify students who are struggling, or who, for a variety of reasons, are considered "at-risk" for learning. Students who are identified as at-risk through the Tier 1 screening process are provided with additional Tier 2 support.

Tier 2 interventions are targeted for a specific group of students. A small group of students with a similar academic need are grouped together to receive more focused academic support. Tier 2 interventions are provided *in addition to* the general education curriculum. Tier 2 interventions and supports are not designed to replace general education instruction and curriculum. In primary school (kindergarten-third grade), these small groups are typically focused on basic reading or math skills. Tier 2 interventions are generally provided for extended periods of time to allow for sufficient time for growth.

Tier 3 interventions consist of individual and more intense support to students who did not achieve sufficient growth with first- and second-tiered interventions. Students who do not show sufficient growth at this individual level of support or who do not "respond to intervention" are typically referred for a comprehensive evaluation to be considered eligible for special education.

The RTI framework is designed to identify and provide targeted interventions for "at-risk" students to reduce special education referrals from schools and to prevent overidentifying students with special education disabilities if they do not have a disability. However, while schools may be required to move through the tiers in a sequential manner, parents can request the school to conduct a special education evaluation at any time.

Providing support for students with academic differences requires collaboration among the professionals in the schools and the adults at home. No one single person is solely responsible for identifying the specific needs of students, planning interventions and strategies to support student needs, and implementing strategies. Together, educators, administrators, and parents must collaborate and agree to what areas of need should be targeted and what interventions and strategies will be used to support students.

Who Is Best Prepared to Implement Interventions and Strategies?

Before discussing how to support students' needs, it is important to discuss who is best prepared to provide the support students require. General education teachers, special education teachers, and service providers must each have unique preparation to work together to implement interventions and classroom strategies.

General Educator

General education teachers are responsible for providing universal instruction. If a student is struggling, their responsibility is to document the needs of the student. General education teachers can, of course, collaborate with other professionals; however, at the first tier of instruction, they are responsible for implementation instruction. General education teachers are experts in the regular curriculum and grade-level academic standards.

Special Educator

Special education teachers, resource teachers, and inclusion teachers are prepared to collaborate with general education teachers and provide support to students within the general education classroom. Special education teachers are also responsible for managing student individual education programs (IEPs) and monitoring student progress toward IEP goals once a student is identified for a disability. Special educators are the experts of the students' IEPs and the special education process.

Other Service Providers

Other service providers, such as speech language pathologists, occupational therapists, and physical therapists have specific preparation. For example, a speech pathologist is responsible for helping students with communication problems related to speech and language, while a physical therapist would be responsible for helping students with limitations related to motor movements. Other service providers are expected to collaborate and consult with general education teachers and special education teachers to provide support and guidance to meeting the student's needs. Depending on the level of student needs, these services may be provided one-to-one or in small groups outside the general education classroom. Other service providers are responsible for addressing the needs of students with IEPs and are focused on monitoring student progress toward IEP goals relevant to their expertise.

Differentiated Academic Support for Students in General Education Classrooms

Differentiated instruction is an approach to teaching that factors students' individual learning styles and levels of readiness *before* designing a lesson plan. Differentiated instruction may mean the teacher will teach the same material to all students using a variety of instructional strategies, or differentiated instruction may require the teacher to deliver lessons at varying levels of difficulty based on the ability of each student. Teachers who practice differentiation in the classroom may: design lessons based on students' learning styles; manage the classroom to create a safe and supportive environment for all students; and continually assess and adjust lesson content to meet students' changing needs. In the following sections, we will examine interventions that address executive functioning, reading, written expression, mathematics, and communication.

> *Differentiated instruction may be teaching the same material to all students using a variety of instructional strategies.*

Executive Functioning

Direct instruction (also called direct teaching or explicit instruction) helps to address executive functioning skills of attention to tasks and working memory deficits, which impact students' ability to follow directions (Sadeghi & Pourhaji, 2021; Sweller, 2015). Direct instruction is a way to teach in a structured way and provides pacing intended to meet the needs of all students. According to Watson and Slocum (2003), *direct instruction* has three elements:

1. **Clear communication of program design** that identifies the "big ideas" to be taught (concepts, rules, strategies). The program design includes a scripted presentation that provides consistent language, the structure of how the skill will be taught, and what supports will be used to teach the skill. As students become more efficient in the tasks, less support is given to allow students to build self-efficiency.
2. **Instruction** is broken down into four components; (a) organize students into groups to meet the needs of students with similar academic needs;
(b) allocate sufficient time and use time well; (c) implement the program; and (d) engage in continuous assessment of students' skills and abilities.
3. **Student-teacher interactions** emphasize the importance of knowing what will motivate students by understanding them as individuals and knowing the student's skills and adjusting instruction based on student progress.

Reading

Reading includes basic reading skills and decoding and reading comprehension. Reading is a highly researched topic because it is considered the building block of learning. Many reading interventions and strategies are introduced at the primary school level (grades K–2) when students are learning to read. However, students who do not acquire reading skills at the primary level will benefit from reading interventions at the intermediate level through secondary school levels (i.e., grades 3–12). In this section, we discuss reading interventions to help students who need reading support. Students who have difficulty applying phonics skills to new or novel words will find it difficult to decode, or accurately read, new words, which can in turn impact reading comprehension.

Basic reading interventions target reading skills such as understanding letter-sound relationships and sight word recognition. Letter-sound and word analysis are prereading skills that involve the grapheme (letter) and phoneme (sound) relationships, also known as phonics. Phonics are the building blocks to reading new words. *Multisensory methods* can be used to teach prereading skills. Images of the word colors, reading aloud, and shapes are examples of multisensory approaches to use in letter-sound and word analysis teaching activities. The multisensory method to prereading, where the instructor says the letter aloud, writes the letter for students to see, and touches the letter shapes has been shown to improve the reading skills of students in early elementary school grades (Widyana et al., 2020). Although the flashcard method can also be used to teach phonics skills, the multisensory approach shows significant gains for students (Phillips & Feng, 2012).

Sight word recognition refers to the skill of being able to identify words correctly on sight, or automatically, without the use of letter-sound skills or word-analysis skills. *Incremental rehearsal* interventions support sight word reading fluency with flashcards of known and unknown words (Wright, 2013). As students gain mastery of unknown words, the cards are moved to the known pile until the student knows all words on the list. Decks of cards are usually comprised of 10 flashcards. Students are shown each flashcard, and if the correct word is not produced within 2–3 seconds, the word is documented as an "unknown" word. The person conducting the intervention then pronounces each "unknown" word as it goes into the unknown pile. As students gain mastery of the list by correctly reading the words, the flashcard is moved to the "known" pile. Using this type of method provides an easy way to collect baseline data and progress monitoring data by counting and documenting which words were "known" and "unknown" at the end of each intervention session. The use of flashcard interventions can be as physical flashcards, digital, or virtual flashcards.

Reading comprehension interventions target students' ability to understand written language through decoding of text that was read, making connections between what they read and being able to make inferences or predictions about what was read. Direct instruction, as discussed in the executive functioning section, is also appropriate to support reading comprehension skills. For example, if a science teacher starts a new section on amphibians, the teacher would first *introduce* students to what amphibians look like by showing a short video about the different types of amphibians. Next, the teacher would *present* the students with new definitions related to amphibians, such as reptile, vertebrate, or cold-blooded. Students would then complete a whole class *guided practice* exercise to distinguish amphibians from other types of animals (i.e., mammals, birds, reptiles). The teacher would provide *feedback* throughout the lesson to reinforce concepts. Students would then complete an *independent practice* exercise. During independent practice, students attempt to accomplish the assignment steps, independently, without support; however, teachers can still provide feedback and corrections as needed. Afterward, the teacher will *assess* student independent practice to determine if further instruction is needed or if the group can move on to the next step.

Reading comprehension is influenced by prior knowledge of vocabulary and concepts. Strong reading comprehension skills are especially important in later elementary through middle school, and developing these skills in early elementary school will help students succeed in higher grades (Eason et al., 2012). As students progress through school, the types of questions and the cognitive skills necessary for reading change (Eason et al., 2012). *Cognitive strategies*, or strategies that guide thinking and information processing, help to support reading comprehension development. One example of cognitive strategy is called the Ask-Read-Tell (Table 9.1), or ART, strategy (McCallum et al., 2010). ART engages interest, accesses prior knowledge, and provides opportunities for students to ask clarifying questions. The ART strategy involves three steps: (1) ASK what the topic is likely

TABLE 9.1 Reading Comprehension Strategy: Example of ASK-READ-TELL Form

Step	Check
Step 1: ASK	Before I read, I will ask myself these questions based on the title of the passage: • What is the main topic? What is it about? • What information do I already know about this topic? • What are two questions I would like to answer in my reading? 1. _____ 2. _____
Step 2: READ	I will read the passage carefully and check for full understanding: • While reading, I will stop after each paragraph to ask, "Did I understand what I read?" • If I do understand, I will mark it with a check (+). If I do not understand, I will mark it with a minus (–) and: ✓ Read it again ✓ Slow my reading ✓ Focus my full attention on reading ✓ Underline any words I do not know and try to figure them out by reading (context) or finding their meaning (dictionary, other resource).
Step 3: TELL	Based on my reading, here are the answers to my two questions: 1. _____ 2. _____ Other interesting information:

to be and generate two questions the student hopes to answer through reading; (2) READ each paragraph and stop to determine whether they understand the section, allowing for clarification; and (3) TELL what you have learned by answering the questions that the student generated.

Graphic organizers may also be used to support reading comprehension and can include concept maps, Venn diagrams, or story maps. A useful feature of graphic organizers is that they can be applied to different text structures and can be used in any subject (writing, science, math, literature, or social studies). *Summarization strategies* provide a structure for telling what the text is about in a concise manner by concentrating on the main points of the text (Watson et al., 2012). The four components, or steps, of summarization are: (1) identify or formulate main ideas; (2) connect main ideas; (3) identify or delete redundancies; and (4) restate the main ideas and connections using different words or phrases.

Written Expression

Written expression has three core domains: expressive language, mechanics, and handwriting. In primary school, written expression interventions typically focus on writing mechanics, on handwriting, and on early expressive language skills, like building vocabulary. Intermediate school and secondary schools typically focus on more complex and demanding writing tasks that involve expressive language.

Writing mechanics refers to the technical aspects of writing like spelling, punctuation, capitalization, and abbreviations. Writing mechanics involve long-term memory and retrieval, meaning students have to remember and apply the rules for writing mechanics. For spelling, *direct instruction* that provides explicit steps in sound-symbol relationships and word patterns has been found to be effective (Williams et al., 2017). *Self-regulated strategy development*, also referred to as *strategy instruction* (Gillespie & Graham, 2014), can also incorporate writing mechanics, including punctuation and spelling. Another helpful strategy for supporting students to remember the steps of writing mechanics, or rules of writing, is to provide *visual supports*. Visual supports for writing can include images of punctuation and what they mean, when and how to abbreviate words, and when to capitalize.

Handwriting interventions often focus on fine motor skills. Interventions that include *handwriting practice* are found to be effective (Hoy et al., 2011) for students with poor writing skills. Some interventions for handwriting problems may include removing handwriting as a barrier and allowing students to use technology. For example, using *talk to text* or other dictation methods converts the spoken word into text and takes the pressure off the writing mechanics. It allows for students to solely focus on generating ideas.

Written Expression refers to the ideas that are being presented in writing and includes grammar. *Self-regulated strategy development* (Gillespie & Graham, 2014) is a writing strategy that helps students move along a three-phase model of writing. In the Forethought Phase, students set a goal that serves as encouragement to focus on positive outcomes and to increase motivation and engagement in the task. In the Performance Phase, students self-monitor, which allows them to practice what was modeled and to check their progress on scaffolded steps to meet their goals. Students in the Self-Reflection Phase evaluate their writing and receive feedback from their peers and teachers. Feedback can *reinforce* connections between the strategy and successful completion of the task.

Additionally, *graphic organizers* (Figure 9.1) provide visual and spatial displays that are common tools used to help students plan and organize their thoughts (Hughes et al., 2019). Computer-based *graphic organizers* are designed to provide the visual and spatial displays of the traditional paper graphic organizers.

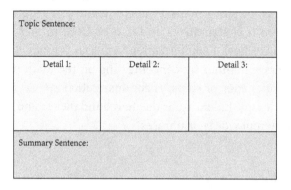

FIGURE 9.1 Written expression strategy: Example of graphic organizer for writing a paragraph.

Mathematics

Math skills include two primary domains: basic math skills like number sense and calculation, and problem-solving skills. Basic math skills are often addressed in primary school, and problem-solving skills are most often addressed in intermediate school to secondary school.

Basic math skills include counting, understanding amounts, sizes, distance, and other forms of descriptive measurement. Students must be able to remember basic math facts and how to apply them. *Incremental rehearsal intervention* builds math fact fluency by pairing known items with unknown items (Lemke et al., 2012) and can be taught with math fact flashcards or with computer-based programs that can be purchased by a school or district. *Multisensory approaches* are also useful for math instruction, and they engage students by allowing them to experience instruction through sight when a teacher models the instruction; sound, when students hear the teacher's verbal instruction; and touch, when students are able to use manipulatives and physical objects.

Math problem-solving involves the ability to access prior knowledge, the ability to keep in mind images, or the representations, of information that has been presented, the ability to choose an appropriate strategy to solve novel problems. *Cognitive strategies* can support math problem-solving skills because they put emphasis on comprehension, representation, and planning (Montague et al., 2014). One type of cognitive strategy is called Solve It! (Montague et al., 2014), which breaks down problem solving into steps:

1. **Reading.** Reading and rereading to identify relevant and irrelevant information.
2. **Paraphrasing.** Encouraging students to put concepts into their own words without changing the meaning.
3. **Visualizing.** Transforming the information to a representation that shows the relationship between all the different parts of the problem.

4. **Hypothesizing.** Predicting which strategy, number of steps, or function will be needed to complete the problem.
5. **Estimating.** Predicting the outcome based on the question.
6. **Computing.** Implementing the strategy and calculating the solution.
7. **Checking.** Reviewing for accuracy the process, strategies, and computation.

Communication

Communication refers to expressive and receptive language skills, both written and oral. In this section, we discuss listening comprehension and oral expression, which involves spoken or oral language. Listening comprehension and oral expressive skills typically begin being addressed in preschool and primary school and can be targeted throughout students' academic years. Consider how much teachers rely on oral language. How is academic instruction provided? How are behavior expectations conveyed? How is collaboration between teachers and students typically conducted? Children who face challenges in communication and language may miss out on key instruction. These students will struggle to learn new concepts and will have limited opportunities to work with their peers.

Listening comprehension involves processing spoken language and includes understanding vocabulary, grammar, and narratives of others when they speak. Language processing refers to the ability to create mental images of the words being spoken. Providing *visuals* can reduce the cognitive load of trying to process oral information by connecting the oral information with a visual concept. *Direct instruction* and *metacognitive strategies* have also been shown to support listening comprehension. *Metacognitive strategies* are strategies that help learners think about their own thinking and provide a structure for understanding spoken language. Below is an example of a four-step metacognitive strategy (Richards, 2016):

1. **Assess Prior Knowledge.** What do I already know about the topic, what resources do I have, and what are the barriers I may face before engaging in the task?
2. **Monitor.** How effective is my performance right now? Am I accomplishing the task?
3. **Self-evaluate.** How effective was my performance? Did I accomplish the task?
4. **Self-testing.** If I use the same resources and skills, will I come up with the same response? Am I able to accomplish the task again?

Oral expression strategies target a student's ability to demonstrate their knowledge or express ideas through oral language. Students must have knowledge of vocabulary and grammar to communicate their ideas effectively. For students with less severe oral expression needs, other methods can be used to help support students' ability to demonstrate their understanding or communicate their thoughts. *Visuals graphics* can be used as an alternative to verbal expression. Other strategies for oral expression may involve *pre-teaching* or *practicing,* which allows for students to be prepared to engage in classroom discussions by being introduced to the topic or concept ahead of time and being given time to prepare. It is also recommended to allow students to give permission, or volunteer, to provide responses aloud to avoid embarrassing the student. Like with written expression, *direct instruction, self-regulated strategy development or strategy instruction,* and *graphic organizers* may be used to teach oral expression in the general education classroom. However, unlike written expression which uses talk-to-text, students with stronger written expression skills can use *text-to-speech* to communicate and practice their oral expression skills.

Ice Cream   Music   Computer   Toy

FIGURE 9.2 Oral expression strategy: Example of picture.

For students with more severe oral expression needs, *augmentative and alternative communication (AAC)* supports the development of communication skills. Picture Exchange Communication System (PECS) is an icon-based form of AAC and is most used by students with autism spectrum disorder (Ganz et al., 2012) to help them communicate with others. However, PECS can be used by students who have no verbal skills or have extremely limited ability to communicate using spoken language. PECS is a multisensory approach that uses sight, sound, and touch to teach students how to communicate their wants, needs and thoughts.

PECS training occurs in six phases:

1. **Initial Communication Training** is typically done by creating an icon of a reinforcer (Figure 9.2), which is a preferred item or activity. The student is presented with the reinforcer and the icon. When the student reaches for the reinforcer, the icon is placed in their hand by the communication partner who guides the student's hand and places it in the communication partner's other hand. Once the communication partner has the icon in their hand, they give the reinforcer to the student. After a few seconds, the reinforcer is taken away and repeated until the student consistently and independently hands the icon to the communication partner to gain the reinforcer.

2. **Retrieval and Delivery of Icons.** Students are taught to independently retrieve and deliver an icon to a communication partner who is not within their immediate vicinity. Depending on student ability, this could mean traveling to a different room or a location within the room if they are physically able to do so. Students could also use a nonverbal indicator, like a learned gesture (raising hand, putting up two fingers), to gain the communication partner's attention.

3. **Icon and Item Discrimination.** At the third phase, the student is presented with two icons. One of the icons is of a reinforcer and an icon of something that is not desired by the student. If the student hands the icon of something that is not desired or preferred by the student, they are given that item or activity. When the student shows disinterest in the undesirable icon that the student selected, the communication partner takes it away. The communication partner will then reintroduce the reinforcer with the icon of the reinforcer. However, if the student does choose the correct icon, they are presented with the reinforcer and provided with social reinforcement (verbal praise).

4. **Phrases.** The next phase introduces sentence strips with the beginning of phrases. For example, "I WANT ..." The student is taught to combine the sentence strip with the icon for the reinforcer and then give the sentence to the communication partner to receive the reinforcer.

The communication partner responds by saying the sentence aloud and then presenting the student with the reinforcer.

5. **Answering Questions.** In this phase, to earn the reinforcers, the communication partner will teach the student how to respond to prompt by asking a question like, "What do you want?" The reason for asking the student a question is to encourage the student to use the "I WANT" sentence strip with the reinforcer icon. When the student does use the "I WANT" phrase appropriately, the communication partner responds by giving the reinforcer to the student.

6. **Commenting.** During the commenting phase, students are presented with sentence strips that include statements like "I SEE" and "I HEAR." Students are taught to use the sentence strips to comment on their environment.

Summary

Throughout this chapter, interventions and strategies have been introduced that can support students with disabilities within and across content areas by targeting specific characteristics or areas of need. Additionally, each strategy features one or more of the UDL principles introduced in Chapter 6: Representation, Engagement, and Action and Expression. These strategies are recommended for use in addition to the general education curriculum and instruction. These strategies are not meant to replace general education instruction. Although this chapter focuses on academic skills, it is important to acknowledge the role behavior and relationships with teachers play in student academic success. Student relationships and connectiveness in the school is also an important factor for academic success.

Test Your Knowledge

Consider the information presented in this chapter and answer the following questions:

1. What will your future role be in implementing interventions?
2. What skills do you already possess to implement the intervention?
3. What challenges might you encounter when implementing academic interventions for students with disabilities?
4. What are the drawbacks of your role in implementing interventions?

Apply Your Knowledge

Complete the Universal Design for Learning Lesson Plan Outline

1. Choose an academic need in a student which you would like to address or improve.
2. Determine if you will be targeting an individual student (Tier 2) or a small group of students with similar needs (Tier 3).
3. Then choose an intervention or strategy that would likely address the need you have chosen.
4. Apply the principles of Representation, Engagement, and Action and Expression of **UDL** to a lesson plan to accommodate for students' needs.

5. Create instructional materials to use in your lesson plan. Your materials must reflect the principles of representation, action and expression, and engagement.

6. In the modifications and adaptations section of the lesson plan, provide at least one example indicating how you intend to change instructional materials to address representation, action and expression, and engagement specifically to meet the academic need identified that you intend to target.

Universal Design for Learning Lesson Plan Outline

Lesson Plan Topic and Grade Level:

Developed By:

Target Student(s):

IEP Goal
IEP Annual Goal for Students with Disabilities   Student name(s):   IEP goals: At the end of _____ the student will be able to _____ with _____ accuracy

Lesson Objectives
Central Focus   Student(s) will understand:

Academic Standard

Materials		
Representation	**Action and Expression**	**Engagement**

Article References

Methods
Lesson Format   **Introduction**

Procedure	Teacher will ...	Student will ...
Attending Cue (to gain student attention)		
Anticipatory Set (preassessment, review, or new information?)		

Body

Procedure	Teacher will ...	Student will ...
Input (methods and techniques, link to prior learning):		
Modeling (demonstration, video, verbal explanation):		
Guided Practice (prompts, corrective feedback):		
Independent Practice (students demonstrate skill):		

Closure

Assessment			
Student	Exceeds Expectations	Meets Expectations	Approaching Expectations
Student will ...			

Modifications and Adaptions		
Representation	Action and Expression	Engagement

(Adapted from Courey et al., 2012)

References

Eason, S., Goldberg, L., Young, K., Geist, M. C., & Cutting, L. (2012). Reader-text interactions: How differential text and question types influence cognitive skills needed for reading comprehension. *Journal of Educational Psychology, 104*(3), 515–528.

Courey, J., Tappe, P., Siker, J., & LePage, P. (2012). Improved lesson planning with universal design for learning (UDL). *Teacher Education and Special Education, 36*(1), 7–27, doi: 10.1177/0888406412446178

Ganz, J., Simpson, R., & Lund, E. (2012). The Picture Exchange Communication System (PECS): A promising method for improving communication skills of learnings with autism spectrum disorders. *Education and Training in Autism and Disabilities, 47*(2), 176–186.

Gillespie, A., & Graham, S. (2014). A meta-analysis of writing interventions for students with learning disabilities. *Exceptional Children, 80*(4), 454–473. doi: 10.1177/0014402914527238

Hoy, M., Egan, M., & Feder, K. (2011). A systematic review of interventions to improve handwriting. *Canadian Journal of Occupational Therapy, 78*(1), 13–25. https://doi.org/10.2182/cjot.2011.78.1.3

Hughes, M., Regan, K., & Evmenova, A. (2019). A computer-based graphic organizer with embedded self-regulated learning strategies to support student writing. *Intervention in School and Clinic, 55*(1), 13–22. https://doi.org/10.1177/1053451219833026.

Lemke, E., Hampton, D., & Beyers, S. (2012). Response to interventions in mathematics: Critical elements. *Psychology in the Schools, 49*(3), 257–272. doi: 10.1002/pits.21596

McCallum, R. S., Krohn, K. R., Skinner, C. H., Hilton-Prillhart, A., Hopkins, M., Waller, S., & Polite, F. (2010). Improving reading comprehension of at-risk high-school students: The art of reading program. *Psychology in the Schools, 48*(1), 78–86.

Montague, M., Krawec, J., Enders, C., & Dietz, S. (2014). The effects of cognitive strategy instruction on math problem solving of middle-school students of varying ability. *Journal of Educational Psychology, 106*(2), 469–481. doi: 10.1037/a0035176

Phillips, W., & Feng, J. (2012). Methods for sight word recognition in kindergarten: Traditional flashcard method vs. multisensory approach. [Paper Presentation]. Annual Conference of the Georgia Educational Research Association, Savannah, Georgia.

Response to Intervention Action Network. (n.d.). What is RTI? Retrieved from http://www.rtinetwork.org/learn/what/whatisrti

Richards, J. (2016, January 15). *Teaching listening #5–listening strategies: Cambridge English*. World of Better Learning | Cambridge University Press. Retrieved August 15, 2022, from https://www.cambridge.org/elt/blog/2016/01/15/teaching-listening-5-listening-strategies/

Sadeghi, M., & Pourhaji, M. (2021). The contributions of working memory and pre-task explicit instruction to L2 oral performance. *System 96*. https://doi.org/10.1016/j.system.2020.102409

Sweller, J. (2015). Working memory, long-term memory, and instruction design. *Journal of Applied Research in Memory and Cognition, 5*(4), 360–367. https://doi.org/10.1016/j.jarmac.2015.12.002

U.S. Department of Education (U.S. DOE). (2006). IDEA regulations: Alignment with the no child left (NLBC) act. Retrieved from https://sites.ed.gov/idea/files/Alignment_with_NCLB_2-2-07.pdf

U.S. Department of Education (U.S. DOE). (2007). No child left behind: Help for students and their families. Retrieved from https://www2.ed.gov/parents/academic/involve/2006toolkit/nclb-en.html

Watson, S., Gable, R., Gear, S., & Hughes, K. (2012). Evidence-based strategies for improving reading comprehension of secondary students: Implications for students with learning disabilities. *Learning Disabilities Research and Practice, 27*(2), 79–89.

Watkins, C, & Slocum, T. A. (2003). Elements of Direct Instruction. *Journal of Direct Instruction, 3,* 4-32.

Widyana, R., Astuti, K., Bahrussofa, M., & Simanjuntak, G. (2020). The effectiveness of Jolly Phonics and multisensory learning methods in improving preschool reading skills. *International Journal of Innovation, Creativity, and Change, 11*(8). Retrieved from https://www.ijicc.net/images/vol11iss8/11801_Widyana_2020_E_R.pdf

Williams, K., Walker, M., Vaughn, V., & Wanzek, J. (2017). A synthesis of reading and spelling interventions and their effects on spelling outcomes for students with learning disabilities. *Journal of Learning Disabilities, 50*(3), 286–297. doi: 10.1177/0022219415619753

Wright, J., (2013). How to build sight-word vocabulary: 4 methods. Retrieved from https://www.interventioncentral.org/sites/default/files/pdfs_blog/instruction_reading_vocabulary_sight_words_acquisition_4_methods.pdf

Figure Credits